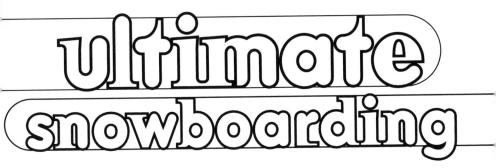

ultimate
snowboarding

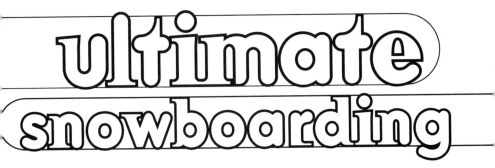

Bethany Stevens

editor, *Fresh and Tasty* magazine

CB

CONTEMPORARY BOOKS

Library of Congress Cataloging-in-Publication Data

Stevens, Bethany.
    Ultimate snowboarding / Bethany Stevens.
       p.   cm.
    Includes index.
    ISBN 0-8092-2969-2
    1. Snowboarding.   I. Title.
    GV857.S57S83   1998
    796.9—dc21   97-43789
                                   CIP

Photo on p. xv by John Grinter. Photos on pages xix, 4, 7, 10, 51, 67, 68–69, 70, 74–77, 86–89, 95, 98, and 121 copyright © Patty Segovia/Silver Photo Agency. Photos on p. 6 (left) and 47 courtesy of K2 Snowboards. Photos on pages 6 (right), 18, 32, 33, 34 (top), 35, 36 (top), and 44 courtesy of Burton Snowboards. Photos on pages 9, 12, 17, 56, 57, 63, 71, 78–85, 90–93, 106, 114, 119, and 126–127 copyright © Gary Land. Photo on page 23 by John Roskoski, courtesy of Barfoot Snowboards. Photo on page 25 courtesy of Mervin Manufacturing. Photo on page 26 by Jay Grell. Photos on pages 34 (bottom), 36 (bottom), 37, and 45 courtesy of Airwalk. Photo on page 111 copyright © MCMXCVII Skye Chalmers. Photo on page 128 copyright © W. Bacon, Science Source/Photo Researchers.

Cover design by Todd Petersen
Cover photograph copyright © by Gary Land
Interior design and production by Susan H. Hartman

Published by Contemporary Books
An imprint of NTC/Contemporary Publishing Company
4255 West Touhy Avenue, Lincolnwood (Chicago), Illinois 60646-1975 U.S.A.
Copyright © 1998 by Bethany Stevens
Printed in the United States of America
International Standard Book Number: 0-8092-2969-2
18   17   16   15   14   13   12   11   10   9   8   7   6   5   4   3   2   1

Contents

Preface

In 1995 I created *Fresh and Tasty* magazine out of a desire to inspire women by featuring female role models actively involved in the amazing new sport of snowboarding. Not feeling encouraged and inspired by the male athletes, I looked to other women snowboarders to show me the possibilities. I wanted a magazine that showed women participating in the action, not just standing by on the sidelines. By reviewing equipment, keeping our readers up to date on the latest and greatest products, interviewing the seasoned pros and keeping an eye out for the budding ones, *Fresh and Tasty* has been tracking the evolution of this delicious new sport.

But . . . whenever the snow melted, and I would rejoin the nonsnowboarding world, I was always surprised by the number of people who still didn't know anything about snowboarding. Because I was so immersed in it, I assumed everyone knew that you stand sideways on a snowboard, that snowboarding is allowed at almost all ski resorts, and that snowboarding is going to be a full medal event in the 1998 Winter Olympics in Nagano, Japan. *Ultimate Snowboarding* is a response to this lack of information. *Fresh and Tasty* is for the snowboarding enthusiast, but there are still many who don't know about this wonderful sport. *Ultimate Snowboarding* introduces snowboarding to the soon-to-be enthusiast—no experience needed.

Since snow is the operative word here, and there are so many words that have been developed to refer to the wonderful joy of snow, such as pow, fluff, freshies, stashes—anything you can think of that sounds like yummy, delicious powder—why don't you put on your hat and mittens and grab some hot cocoa to set the mood.

This is the story of snowboarding.

Acknowledgments

I would like to thank Gary Land, Patty Segovia, John Grinter, and Skye Chalmers for adding clarity and beauty to *Ultimate Snowboarding* with their photos. Photographing snowboarding is a tough job. Photographers typically have to give up first tracks, suffer intolerable cold for that perfect picture, and snowboard while weighted down by heavy camera equipment so that we can sit on our couches and admire the beauty of winter.

I also would like to thank Melissa Longfellow, the copublisher of *Fresh and Tasty*. If it were not for her willingness to take risks and her confidence in our ability, *Fresh and Tasty* might have never become a reality.

I owe many thanks to my mother, Linda Calligaro (for, of course, giving me life and for the typical motherly care and nurture), who tirelessly edited my work. I'm sure she saved my copyeditor endless hours.

I thank my agent, Dan Mandel, for believing I could do this.

And, of course, my husband, Jack. It is with him that I discovered snowboarding, and it is to him that I owe many fresh powder days. Working hard to help support my pursuits in snowboarding, Jack is snowboarding's number-one fan . . . and I'm his number-one fan.

Introduction

It's April 11, 1996, and I am driving home from Jay Peak, Vermont. A record fall of three feet was shared by me, five friends, and forty-seven others. The day was spent trying to be the first through the stashes of fresh snow, all of us unable to believe that spring had already sprung. Travis pointed his nose straight for the fence jump (the catwalk drops down to the trail, making a perfect takeoff with a steep, powdery landing). Hoping to mark his takeoff to avoid the "No Jumping" signs, he managed to pull off a 360. Not too shabby. I chose a nice conservative air, lofting high and landing in the powder. Then Jack came down with a huge frontside 180, hitting the jump switch and landing regular. He dropped it at the top of the fence, diagonally, and landed into the deepest fluff of all. With everyone hooting and hollering, we straight-lined down to the lift to do it again.

Every winter my boyfriend, Jack, and I would spend a couple of weekends skiing. He was an excellent skier, very aggressive and very fast. I was much more timid. I didn't feel very strong on the independent floating sticks of wood, and I was nervous about falling on those poles that I wasn't sure what to do with anyway. I forever felt like one leg could go one way, the other leg in the opposite direction, and my arms would be caught up in the pole straps. The best solution was to ditch skiing altogether and choose something neither of us had done so that we could start on equal ground. Then I would have an equal chance and not always be lagging behind, careening down the mountain after him thinking, "If I fall right now, it would really hurt."

Jack's initial reaction was, "I don't want to snowboard. Snowboarders are a bunch of punks, ruining all the snow on the mountain. Skiing rules!" But after some gentle persuasion and a tape recorder left under his bed at night— "Skiing baaaad, snowboarding goood. Skiing baaaad, snowboarding goooood"—he decided to give it a try. That was four years, and over 250 snowboarding days, ago.

Snowboarding is unlike any other sport I have ever tried. It is so satisfying and so enjoyable simply because you rely on yourself and a single piece of wood. Nothing else to get the credit for performing so beautifully. With this independence is freedom, and with that freedom is confidence.

You're also communing with nature. Taking in an entire mountain, top to bottom. What a beautiful sight! The trees covered with white frosting, the evergreens right out of a Christmas display, the sky clear and blue, and the air so fresh. You can't help but feel awesome.

And the most important part is that snowboarding is really not that hard. Skiing is difficult. It takes strength,

Jillian Sizemore enjoying the back-country of Mt. Baker with Sandy and Nesta

a lot of concentration, and a lot of practice. It's especially difficult because your legs must work independently. When you fall, there is much more to go wrong. The long planks attached to your feet make twisting your knee a strong possibility, especially when you try to avoid landing on the poles. Although snowboarding does require a bit of getting used to, as the sideways stance requires different balancing skills, snowboarding puts all your strength and weight on one edge, on one board. In addition, the wider snowboard stays afloat on varying terrain better than do two skinny skis. And if you're still not convinced, the wider snowboard also allows for a deeper sidecut, which makes for easier turning.

If this is beginning to sound foreign to you, don't worry. We're just getting started, and there's plenty of time to get familiar with this new world of snowboarding. Suffice it to say that you won't be disappointed. The challenge of skiing is just trying to make it down the mountain. Because going down the mountain on a snowboard is so easy, the challenge of snowboarding is maneuvering in between the trees, dropping cliffs, hitting jumps and bustin' it out in the snowboarding park. With this freedom you are able to bring more of your own personal style to your run.

Once you become familiar with the sport and decide to give it a try, schedule a lesson with a professional instructor at your local resort and begin your new adventure. There are videos and magazines, clubs and camps for snowboarding enthusiasts of all ages. And with snowboarding's quick learning curve, you'll soon be looking forward to winter and the many snow days ahead.

Many snowboarding stories will be told during the coverage of the 1998 Winter Olympics, when snowboarding makes its debut. But in order to understand the snowboarding stories, you have to first understand snowboarding. When snowboarding was still virtually unknown in the mid- and late '80s, snowboarding T-shirts were sold listing the "5 Answers." These were the answers

to the five questions most commonly asked by someone
seeing snowboarding for the first time.

1. It's called a snowboard.
2. Yes, it's fun.
3. No, actually it's quite easy.
4. Yes, I can stop it . . . and even turn.
5. No, I don't ski anymore.

Scheduled to be a full-medal sport at the 1998
Olympics in Nagano, Japan, snowboarding could very
possibly attain the same popularity as baseball, football
and basketball. The resorts that still have "No Snowboarding" signs posted can be named on one hand, and
as we get closer to the Olympics you can bet those signs
will come down or be changed to "Welcome Snowboarders." With all the developments in equipment, full-scale
competitions, and groups of people coming together to
push the possibilities, there are bound to be more questions. Although you can't wear these answers to your
questions, you can keep them nearby (neatly organized
in this book), ready to enlighten someone else about this
new sport—snowboarding.

"*I've skied only three times in my life, so I have no idea if crossing over is easier, but having experience in the mountains would be a big plus. Snowboarding has a really fast learning curve—it's an easy sport to pick up. I think that's why so many people get into it and stick with it. I've been involved in a lot of sports, and snowboarding is like no other. I started snowboarding in 1986—that's a lot of winters and a lot of powder turns—and I still can't wait for it to snow again.*"

Tina Basich

Tina Basich lofting a backside method out of the halfpipe

Age: 28

Years snowboarding: 11

Sponsors: Sims, Smith, Airwalk

Focus: Freeriding

How it all began: "In the winter of 1986–87, my brother, Mike, and I rented Burton Elites from the skateboard store. We went to Soda Springs and hiked. We had no idea how the snowboard worked, but we kept at it for a couple of years and soon got the hang of it."

1

What Is Snowboarding?

By now you must have seen snowboarding either at the ski slopes or on television—skiers standing sideways on one board, gracefully carving their way down the snow-covered mountain. The first time snowboarding was introduced to the general population was in the 1985 James Bond movie *A View to a Kill*. Tom Sims (whom you'll meet later) played the stunt double for Roger Moore. Sims was chased by the Russians on his snowmobile, and he craftily hopped sideways onto one of the snowmobile skis and dropped off a huge cliff.

Recently you may have seen snowboarders on ESPN's Winter X Games in 1997 or on MTV Sports. Mountain Dew and MCI have featured snowboarding in commercials to catch the viewer's attention and promote their products. And now, you'll be seeing snowboarding featured as an Olympic event in the 1998 Winter Olympics in Nagano, Japan.

Skiing has been around for over seventy-five years and has thus been shown time and time again in the movies and on television. Many people are familiar with standing forward on two planks and making your way either gracefully and powerfully or timidly and awkwardly (depending on your skill) down the face of the mountain. But what was this? James, you're standing sideways! There's only one board! It looks like they're trying to revive the surfing craze!

What Is Snowboarding?

It's probably easiest to explain snowboarding in relation to skiing. Although the snowboarding story should be told in respect to its roots in surfing and skateboarding rather than as an outgrowth from skiing, the latter makes it a little easier to understand how snowboarding works. Later we can focus on the development of the snowboard itself.

Snowboarding follows the same principle as skiing: steel edges cut into the snow so you can travel down the mountain. And what's skiing? Think adult sledding. Snowboarding is the sideways counterpart to the adult/more advanced form of sledding. And snowboarding is better suited to your anatomy than skiing, making the skill of descending a mountainside even easier to acquire.

Skis are two separate boards that go on each foot; you face forward. A snowboard is ridden sideways with both feet on one board. In skiing, your weight and power are

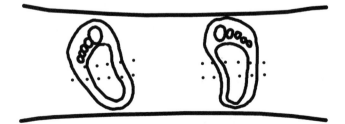

distributed between your two feet, which work independently, whereas in snowboarding all your weight and power are concentrated on one edge, giving you full control. In skiing, the distribution of your weight on the ski is caused by the side to side motion of your foot. In snowboarding, you rock from your toes to your heels to weight the edges—a much more natural position, which gives you better balance.

When skiing you carry poles, but when snowboarding your hands are free. When a skier falls, the equipment releases (called a "yard sale"), but when a snowboarder falls, the snowboard stays attached. While this may sound more dangerous, it is actually safer because you can fall more compactly. Having the snowboard attached to your feet also gives you a better chance to self-arrest by digging the steel edges in and bringing yourself to a stop.

Is Snowboarding Fun?

Snowboarding is all about fun. It's recreation. And why would you choose an unfun recreation? It's skiing (adult sledding) but with ultimate control. What makes it so much fun is the powerful and graceful feeling of turning your way down a snow-covered slope and setting the edge of your snowboard into the powder. Whether in backcountry powder or on resort-groomed trails, the feeling of carving turns is a feeling of power. In addition, it's important to be able to turn, as turning maintains your speed and keeps you from bombing straight down the hill.

And snowboards are easy to turn. The power you experience when being in control brings confidence, which allows you to see the mountain in a whole different light from those skiers who are still struggling to turn. With the skill of getting down the mountain easily mastered, the search is on for bumps, jumps, and obstacles to add to the fun. Confident in your turning abilities, you can now zoom in and out of the trees and even feel comfortable losing contact with the ground to taste the feeling of flying. Your backyard hill begins to look like a snowboarding playground. When the snow begins to fall, memories of childhood days spent sledding come back with the giddy fun of sliding in the snow and falling in a big cloud of powder. Dressed in a warm cocoon, snowboarding reminds you of when your worries were only of a runny nose and whether or not school would be canceled again tomorrow.

Rol Kunkel enjoying the treasures of Whistler

How Does It Work?

The main reason snowboards can turn easily, other than the balanced-sideways stance and toe-heel leverage over the board, is their deep sidecut.

Skis, because they are narrow, can only accommodate a shallow sidecut; and it is the sidecut that directly outlines your turn. Since turning keeps your speed in check, the more you turn, the more control you have. The ski industry is now actually looking at the advantages of snowboard design and incorporating them into their newest, hottest-selling products—Parabolic Skis. These skis are shaped more like a snowboard, with wider tips and tails allowing for a deeper sidecut.

Learning to balance toe-to-heel will take some getting used to, but, once mastered, the sideways stance is a stronger position. Rest assured, balancing skills and the techniques needed to control a snowboard will be taught to you in your first snowboarding lesson. And I guarantee that after your tenth day of snowboarding your skill will surpass that of an equally experienced skier.

Sidecut is the actual cut of the sides of the board as you look down at it.

The wider snowboard also makes riding in the powder much easier, which is the ultimate goal of all snowboarders. Yes, the resort-groomed trails are fun and all, but powder is nirvana. Hiking to the hidden stashes in the trees, trying to find places where no one else has been so you can

Parabolic skis by K2

be the first to leave tracks—that's the source of the ear-to-ear grins. Not only is the backcountry more accessible because your skill on a snowboard is greater, but the size and shape of a snowboard makes riding the powder easier. On skis, powder can be a lot of work, with the weight of the snow making your skis release; you have to maintain perfect technique to stay on top of the snow. On a snowboard, you eas-

Shannon Dunn's signature snowboard by Burton Snowboards

ily ride on top of the snow—the more snow, the more effort-less snowboarding becomes (until you fall—trying to get back up in the deep snow is not quite as graceful as those powder slashes).

What Can You Do on a Snowboard?

The ultimate high for a snowboarder is riding through powder. Unfortunately, most of the time that's up to Mother Nature. So for other forms of an adrenaline rush besides linking graceful turns down the slope, you can fly

Tara Dakides sprayin' a rooster tail

through the air over jumps or search for your own speed limit. There are snowboards and boots designed specifically for those trying to jump the highest and spin the most or for those who feel the need for speed. But most people want to be "free" to do a little bit of everything—thus they are called Freeriders. Freeriders ride the whole mountain laying down carves, looking for knolls to jump, weaving through the trees now and again, and carving, hopping, and jumping their way to the bottom.

About 85 percent of the snowboarding population fit this description, and the other 15 percent focus on one aspect of riding—tricks ("Freestyle") or Mach speed ("Alpine"). Freestylers hang in the local resort's park or hike to the jump they built in the backcountry. Alpine riders are all about going really fast, bashing gates, carving, and racing.

Why Is Riding Style Important?

The equipment available is technologically advanced, allowing you to rule the mountain rather than just participate. The equipment should become an extension of your body, enhancing your performance rather than being just some necessary man-made attachments that get in your way. If you just want to do tricks, a shorter, wider board with less swing weight for easier spinning and stable landings and a twin tip shape so you can ride backward and forward is what you would choose to ride. Racers need a much longer, stiffer, and narrower board that can hold at high speeds, which allows for quick edge changes. Race boards are directional in shape because they are meant to only be ridden facing forward.

But most of the snowboarding population freerides; they look for equipment that will let them do a little of everything. As a beginner it's a good idea to get a freeride setup so you aren't limited to any one style. Specializing

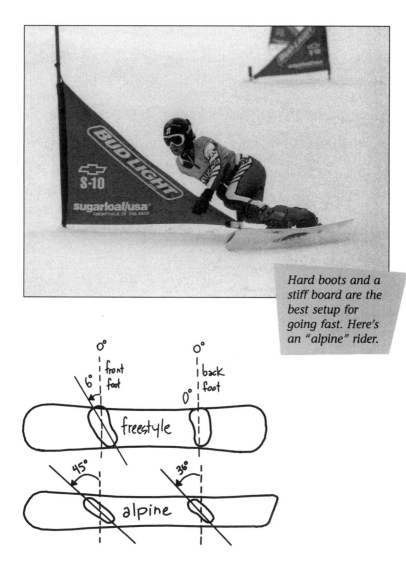

Hard boots and a stiff board are the best setup for going fast. Here's an "alpine" rider.

Cara-beth Burnside is the perfect example of a freestyle rider as she spins this huge 360.

is for the pros or for those who can afford to buy more than one setup. In Chapter 3 I'll provide you with more specifics on snowboarding equipment.

Now let's take a trip to history class for a quick lesson. Before you get into any new sport it is only due respect to know the story of its evolution and give props to those who struggled and forged the path to create such smile-producing fun.

Which type of rider are you?

Although you may see things you like in more than one category, try to decide which category you most identify with.

Freeride: Would you spend your day at the resort searching for the secret stashes of fresh snow? Would you occasionally get the urge to take a few runs through the park but wouldn't spend the day hiking it? Would you get psyched dropping off a cliff or cornice, feeling the earth drop from underneath your feet?

Freestyle: Would you try to do tricks off anything available? Would you spend the day in the park hiking the halfpipe? Would you constantly request that the resort make the jumps bigger? Do you daydream of naming your own trick?

Alpine: Would you spend the day searching for your own speed limit while avoiding the ski patrol, who have been telling you to slow down? Do you gravitate toward the Lycra section of the clothing store? Do you daydream about one day racing in the World Cup?

Ross Powers at 1997's U.S. Open, Stratton, Vermont

Age: 18

Years snowboarding: 10

Sponsors: Burton, Xnix, Swany, Powerbar

Focus: Halfpipe competition, used to race

How it all began: "My mom worked at Bromley in Vermont, near Stratton, so I basically grew up on the mountain. I saw some lift attendants snowboarding, and I wanted to try it. It was something new (this was back in 1987). Skiers didn't really know about snowboarding, and they didn't like the sound of the edges on the ice, but the kids liked it. Bromley had one trail where they let you snowboard."

"**S**ki resorts no longer make you prove to them that you have control, but before snowboarding was accepted you had to get certified. You had to show an instructor that you could turn both ways and stop. If you were good enough, you got 'certified' to go on all the trails."

Ross Powers

2

How Did Snowboarding Begin?

Sports grow and progress in a predictable way. As the technology gets better, the sport becomes more popular, and it becomes easier for people to participate. With more people, more money becomes available, and great things can happen—big contests, better equipment, organized instruction. This is all to the good, and this is what must happen for a sport to mature. But as the group gets bigger, it becomes harder to stay in touch with the center, and the center is where it all began.

Sometimes it's hard to relate to the stories and events that make up a sport's history. But snowboarding's history began a relatively short time ago; that's what makes it so interesting. The people who made snowboarding possible are still involved and very much a presence in the sport. It is because of their vision and hard work that you can now pull into the parking lot of your favorite resort, throw on your warm, stylish clothes and grab your made-for-carving board, filling your pockets with some snacks for the eight-minute chairlift to the top.

Snowboarding and the industry it supports has grown very rapidly. Its development can be understood in the accumulated stories of the past thirty years. Snowboarding is just becoming an "adult," but its childhood is very interesting. Like any child, it has experienced exciting times, disappointments, mistakes, and many, many firsts.

Who Invented Snowboarding?

The official birth of snowboarding is credited to Sherman Poppen. Although other snowboarding figures may argue that they were the first to have the idea of surfing winter's frozen wave, Poppen is the one responsible for the popular Snurfer. Thinking that standing sideways on a piece of wood and descending a snowy slope would be fun, he crudely nailed a piece of wood on top of two skis as a backyard toy for his kids. When Brunswick Sporting Goods, the company he worked for, saw his creation—a stand-up sled—they thought it was a clever enough idea to produce and sell as a winter toy. The Snurfer debuted in 1966 for $15. The design was simple: plywood deck, no bindings, and a rope on the nose—kind of like a single water ski without bindings.

The introduction and acceptance of the Snurfer gave credibility to the idea that it would be fun to stand on a board sideways to ride through the snow. But this sideways-standing winter device was still just a toy. A few who really enjoyed snurfing, along with others who saw the potential from their surfing and skateboarding experiences, began to experiment and push the limits, improving upon and creating better snow-surfing designs.

Looking at a snowboard today, you would think that snowboarding evolved from skiing technology, but it actually grew out of ideas from people who were more interested in increasing the length of their sideways-standing season than in trying to improve their skiing ride. While some drew from their Snurfer experiences and looked to improve the possibilities, others converted their skateboards and surfboards to be snow-compatible. The most commonly heard names in snowboarding's history are Jake Burton Carpenter, Tom Sims, Chuck Barfoot, Dimitrije Milovich, Mike Olson, Jeff Grell, and Steve and

Snurfing, the origin of snowboarding

Dave Derrah. Some of these people came into contact with each other; most were working on their own ideas from their own inspirations. When they did finally come together and saw what each other had done, new ideas developed, and competitive ambition motivated them further. Each one of these great pioneers introduced innovations to snowboarding that made it the sport it is today, allowing snowboarding athletes to push the limits to unbelievable heights.

Some of the improvements that were made included steel edges to dig into the snow's surface, a long enough board to allow you to surf the snow, an exaggerated sidecut to make turning easier, and highback bindings that keep your feet attached and have a "higher back" so the

Jake Burton Carpenter

pressure from your calf helps to initiate heel-side turns. These discoveries transformed snowboarding from merely sliding uncontrollably down a hill to gracefully and skill-fully maneuvering down a mountain. With the snow-board becoming less of an obstacle to overcome and more of an accurate tool, giving you leverage over the snow-covered surface, more people became interested, and snowboarders became hungry for access to more snow. It was time to spread the word that snowboarding was no longer simply a winter diversion, but a new sport.

What Do Snowboarding's Pioneers Have to Say?

JAKE BURTON CARPENTER
Burton Snowboards
1977–present
"I always wanted to surf and had snurfed in the '60s. When I graduated college, I was amazed that no one had pushed the possibilities and improved on the Snurfer idea, so I started my own company in 1977—Burton Boards. When I started the factory, I didn't know anyone else was pursuing the idea, but before I began production, I heard that Dimitrije Milovich was producing Wintersticks in Utah.

"My greatest contribution to snowboarding would be pushing for the growth of the industry. In the early years, I promoted the sport and focused on legitimizing snow-boarding—pushing for its acceptance by ski resorts."

Props: *"Dimitrije Milovich, for being an early innovator and playing around with sidecut; the Derrah brothers, founders of Flite, who worked with the concept of metal edges; Jeff Grell, for the invention of the highback and for using the material* *p-tex on the base of the board. There were a bunch of people playing around all at one time, focusing on their own needs (powder vs. hardpack) and introducing a lot of innovations to make the modern day snowboard."*

TOM SIMS
Sims Snowboards
1977–present

"My early influences were from skiing and skating, back in 1963–64 in South Jersey. I wanted to skateboard on the snowy streets, so I made a 'snowboard' that wasn't much bigger than thirty-five inches. In 1966 I started surfing, and that radically influenced the direction of the boards I was building, making them longer. It was about that time that the Snurfer came on the market. Even though the Snurfer was too narrow, and the rope was geeky, I did see the advantage of the upturned nose. The next big influence was the Mono-ski, which came out in 1969. I thought, 'Everything looks great except they're just standing wrong on the board.' It was then that I built a full-size, solid fiberglass snowboard out of surfboard materials. Surfing still has some influence on snowboard designs today, but snowboarding is its own creature now, influenced purely by snowboarder's needs.

"The first time I became aware of others working on snowboards was in the late '70s, namely, Winterstick and Burton in 1978. Shortly thereafter, Chuck Barfoot was a roommate of mine. The contest scene started picking up in the early '80s, and that's when I really began running into people from the snowboarding 'industry.' At that time, everyone was making tremendous progress monthly. There was no going to trade shows and booking orders in the late spring; we sold directly on the mountains.

"My greatest contribution would be that I built the first board and was the first one to actually ride, really ride, nearly

thirty-five years ago now. Sims, as a company, influenced the freestyle aspect of the sport, introducing the halfpipe and hosting the first halfpipe contest. From the very beginning, I saw snowboarding much more as an independent sport, not just as an adjunct to skiing. Another important contribution is the introduction of the Shannon Dunn model. I met a lot of resistance for featuring a female rider and promoting a women's model—especially from the European countries. It turned out to be a huge hit, and now there is a women's market supplying women-specific hard and soft goods."

Props: "We owe Jake Burton Carpenter a lot for footing the bill and exposing the sport in skiing and surfing mags. Burton Boards has had a profound effect on the growth of the sport. The competitiveness of everybody in this business has pushed us to make a better product. Historically, Dimitrije Milovich was a pioneer in the '70s. His efforts, at the time, were pretty revolutionary. In the early '80s, Mike Olson pioneered the concept of a real sidecut. Neither Burton nor Sims had sidecuts dialed, and Mike Olson came along and pushed them and really created the first carving boards. Chuck Barfoot was working with the Achenbach brothers and developed the first twin tip, which is still a big part of snowboarding today. I give props to Chris and Bev Sanders of Avalanche Snow-boards for their career/lifelong effort to promote snowboard-ing and their loyalty to the sport. There were many people who stuck with this sport for decades, when no money was to be made. The only reason we were involved was for the love of snowboarding."

DIMITRIJE MILOVICH
Winterstick
1975–1980

"Not really a surfer. Grew up in New York, tobogganing and sledding, and it was just natural to try and stand up. Didn't *know Snurfers existed. This guy in New Jersey showed me how to make surf-style boards, so I made some boards and rode some hills covered in snow. At the hill I saw someone with a Snurfer, but it was like a toy. My boards were more similar to a surfboard. I didn't have a rope, just a textured surface so your feet stayed on the board.*

"I hadn't heard of Jake Burton until the 1978 NSGA trade show. We were the only two showing snowboards and no one was talking to us, so we began to talk with each other. From the beginning I knew the importance of designing the snowboard similar to a ski—it had to store energy like a ski or it wouldn't accelerate."

Props: *"Jake Burton and Tom Sims."*

CHUCK BARFOOT
Barfoot Snowboards
1978–present

"In 1962, when I was eleven, my cousin, Randy Barfoot, took me snurfing on the sand in Michigan. But, other than that, I was a surfer and a skater. In 1978 I began working with Sims, building skateboards, and Bob Weber came to Sims to license his plastic ski board. That was the first visual of a snowboard, and I began working with Bob, improving on his ideas and using my workmanship abilities. I took surfboard contour ideas and put them into a snowboard design—a long board. I never had a rope on the nose and used Winterstick's model, which had a swallow tail shape.

"It was at Christmas 1978 in Utah that Bob Weber and I went for my first day of snowboarding. His girlfriend would drive up the road, and we would ride the powder. Later, we ran into a guy on a Snurfer; it was actually Jay Grell of Flite Snowboards, the older brother of the guy who invented the highback. Later that same day Dimitrije Milovich of Winterstick

stopped to talk with me. He was skiing at Snowbird with his niece and tried his boards on the hardpack.

"I'd say my influence was the evolution of shapes that were very functional and are still functional today. I was aiming to make a good powder board, and that's where things are today."

Chuck Barfoot

Props: *"Combination of Sherman Poppen, Dimitrije Milovich, Tom Sims, and Bob Weber."*

MIKE OLSON
Mervin Manufacturing/Gnu Snowboards
1984–present

"I wasn't really influenced by the Snurfer. I was way into skiing and skateboarding. Living in Seattle, I thought it would be cool to be able to skateboard during the winter. In 1977, in my eighth grade shop class, I added metal edges to the skateboards I had already been building and took them to the hardpack to try them out. Thinking that as in skiing, the powder would be more difficult than the hardpack, I tried to stay on the groomed trail, but I accidentally veered off into the powder. It turned so well and felt so good that, on the next day, I decided not to buy a lift ticket but to play with my new invention.

"I had seen Winterstick pictures of Dimitrije Milovich and had also heard of Flite. Winterstick and Flite were my first realizations that snowboarding could exist as a business. I hooked up with a guy who had a bunch of Wintersticks, and after spending the day riding the Wintersticks, I got out my own board and hiked the same hill we had Wintersticked on. I thought my board was much better, and that I should start making snowboards to sell to friends.

"My company, Mervin Manufacturing, made the first carving snowboards that actually had sidecut and camber. If I wanted to make a living selling snowboards, they would have to be compatible with the hardpack, so I eliminated the surfboard fins and added metal edges, like skis. I also realized that snowboards are wide enough to allow for a deep sidecut, and the deep sidecut translates to a carving machine."

Props: *"Dimitrije Milovich from Winterstick and Stevie Derrah from Flite; Chuck Barfoot, who built all the original*

Sims boards. Sims gets credited for the creation of snow-boards, but Chuck was actually making them. Sims was a great rider. Sims was the first guy who really knew how to ride a board."

Mike Olson carving it up even in the summer

Jeff Grell

JEFF GRELL
Inventor of the Hy-Bak (highback)

"Up until 1982–83 people were riding on boards without support. Rubber strap bindings, Velcro, or bungee things were used to hold your boot in place. It was really hard to ride the board without any support, especially on the heel-side edge. My original idea was the highback.

"I originally hooked up with Steve Derrah of Flite Snow-boards. I started riding on his boards back in 1976. He used to have a skateboard company and then he started evolving the Snurfer.

"I'm responsible for a lot of firsts: the first production highback binding in 1985, which I designed with Tom Sims and Dave Weber; the first instructional video for snow-boarding in 1986; the first televised snowboarding event, the 1987 Aspen Grand Prix of Snowboarding; and I started the first snowboarding factory in Royan, France, in 1986."

Props: *"Steve and Dave Derrah of Flite Snowboards deserve a lot of credit. Jake Burton deserves lots of credit for his efforts, but other people who were important early on were Tom Sims and Dave Weber. Chuck Barfoot was a big contributor that I remember real well. Dimitrije Milovich and my brother, Derrek Grell."*

Where Did People Snowboard?

The good ol' days of snowboarding were spent hiking local hills because chairlifts were not an option. A few ski resorts would allow locals access to their hills to try snow-boarding, but as more and more people wanted to try it, the resorts became increasingly reluctant to let their mountains become the practice site for a whole slew of beginners. Almost everyone on a snowboard at this time was a beginner, and their lack of control upset the skiing customers and worried the mountain management. But snowboarders would not give up. Demanding their right to equal access to winter's playground and claiming their money was just as green, snowboarders put the pressure on the resorts to open their doors. Eventually, there were so many people pushing on the doors that they gave in, but at first permission was contingent on demonstrated control of the snowboard and "certification" from the ski resort. Once this was accomplished, snowboarders earned their right to ride the chairlift to the top of the designated snowboarder trail.

The permission to ride the chairlifts opened up snowboarding to a whole new group of people—us lazy recreationers who wouldn't have snowboarded if we had to hike up the mountain first! And with the innovations in board technology and a bit of practice, snowboarders were soon better able to demonstrate control. The beginners were starting to get better, and the ski resorts couldn't help but see dollar signs riding those single boards. Slowly, ski resort after ski resort opened their doors and dropped certification requirements. Gradually, snowboarders were allowed to have access to all the resort's trails, riding the same trails as skiers. Today, there are only five resorts in the United States that are still holding out; the number of snowboarders has risen so dramatically that resorts can no longer ignore them. Because of the declining growth in skiing over the past few years, this spurt of excitement and energy was exactly what the resorts were looking for.

Now, ski resorts are competing with each other to attract snowboarders to their snowboard-friendly mountains by hosting events and dedicating snowboard-only trails, with halfpipes and jumps. Most of the initial tension created by this new sport has begun to subside, and even the skiing customers who were initially upset by the "reckless, cussing, ill-attired menace," as quoted in

Newsweek, have become a little less defensive of their territory and are not stereotyping all snowboarders as "chain-wallet punks."

Is There a Snowboarding Industry?

Snowboarding's potential was undeniable. Here was a sport that offered so much fun, was not that difficult to learn, opened its doors to most who tried, and offered beautiful surroundings. In addition, snowboarding itself was beautiful, which made for limitless media opportunities that piqued the interest of many people, who would then need a snowboard, boots, and clothing.

Enter snowboard manufacturers, who began to supply snowboards, bindings, boots, and clothing. And no sport would be complete without accessories: maintenance kits to care for the bottom of your board, transceivers and shovels to keep you safe from the dangers of playing in the snow, and locks to keep others from trying to snowboard on your board. Not only did snowboarding become a new sport, it also became a new industry.

In 1977 *Powder* magazine ran the first Winterstick ad, and Burton Boards was started. A snowboard-specific magazine premiered in 1985. And by the late '80s there were a handful of snowboard companies showing at the annual ski trade show in Las Vegas, Nevada. With acceptance at the ski resorts, nothing was preventing snowboarding from being introduced to all snow lovers. Demand for snowboards quickly outnumbered supply, and everyone who had a good idea about how to make a snowboard began making their own and starting their own companies. With the tilt in the suppliers' favor, all those in the industry experienced easy success, and by 1994–95 there were more than four hundred snowboard companies offering products for sale. Of course, the market soon became saturated.

Currently, the skiing industry is a $1.6 billion industry, and there are twenty-one ski manufacturers supporting the demand. Snowboarding is only a $400 million industry, yet there are 343 snowboard companies competing for business. Only the companies with exceptional entrepreneurial ability will survive, while others will merge with existing ski companies to weather the long term.

It is inevitable for the excitement to level off and for the growth to become more orderly and predictable. However, that spectacle known as the Olympics will bring even more attention to this fast-growing sport. In addition to the expected growth thanks to the Olympics media blitz, the snowboarding industry is also counting on taking over skiing's customers. Currently in the United States there are only 3.7 million snowboarders, yet there are 10.4 million skiers.

From an industry standpoint, this is a great plan, but it does create problems for the snowboarder trying to get first tracks. It is always a controversy: the growth of the industry leads to increased population competing for snow space. And the inevitable free spirit versus the organization thing. In whose hands will snowboarding ultimately rest as it reaches adulthood? Those passionate about snowboarding or those passionate about business? One thing is sure: there is no longer a question regarding snowboarding's acceptance—that goal has been achieved.

3

What Do You Need to Snowboard?

What do you need to snowboard? Not much. Snowboarding does not require a lot of equipment. I know that I'm sounding a little biased here as I continue to sing the praises of snowboarding, but it's so simple and so much fun. Even the equipment is simple. You, of course, need a snowboard, as well as something to attach the snowboard to your feet, something to wear on your feet, and, since snowboarding is a winter sport, clothing to keep you warm and dry. There is a lot of information in this section, so let's get right to it.

Equipment decisions are based on the size of the rider and the desired riding style. As I mentioned in Chapter 1, there are three different riding styles that reflect three different goals: to go as fast as possible, to do as many tricks as possible, or to do a little of both but not to the extreme.

Those who want to go as fast as possible belong in the "alpine" category. The goal of the alpine setup is to help you obtain the best transfer of energy from yourself to the board, making for the most efficient use of the "machine" on your feet. Alpine riders wear ski-like hard boots, ride stiff, narrow boards, and place their feet less than shoulder width apart, pointing their toes toward the nose of the board. The hard boots allow no "mush," or energy loss, and the narrow, forward stance maximizes the use of the

Alpine snowboard

Alpine binding

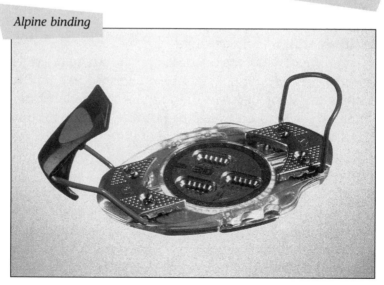

quadriceps for leverage on the edges of the snowboard. A narrow board allows for quick edge changes.

"Freestyle" riders are all about jumping higher while spinning and posing in the air. Typically, freestyle riders wear whatever is the most stylish: comfortable outfits and soft sneaker-looking boots. They attach the board to their feet with straps and set their stance at least shoulder width apart, placing their feet closer to 90 degrees across the board. The advantage of the soft boots is that they allow for maximum flexibility when attempting to

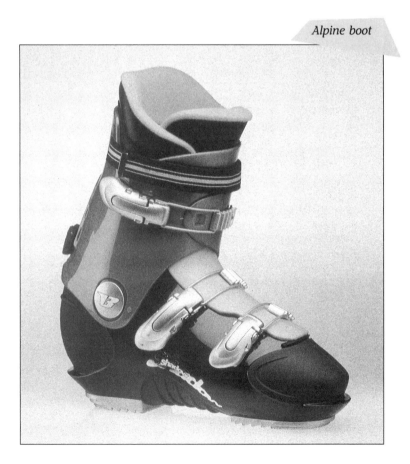

Alpine boot

"pose" in the air. The wide board allows for stable landings and accommodates a true sideways stance. The
shorter overall length makes for quick spinning.

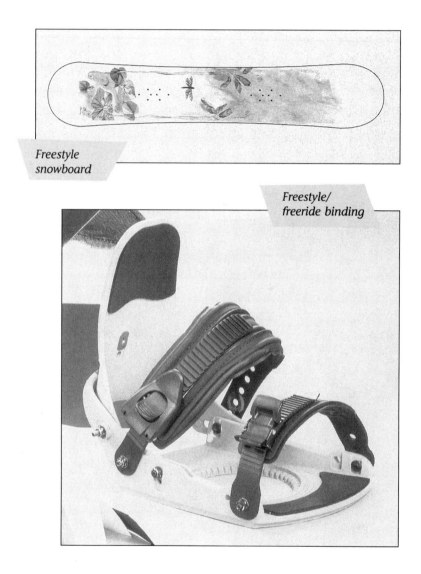

*Freestyle
snowboard*

*Freestyle/
freeride binding*

If you're not all about jumping or all about going fast, then you belong in the "freeride" group. Freeride is a combination of these styles. Freeriders don't want to specialize in one type of riding but would rather ride a little of everything. Therefore, freeride boards are not extreme in their proportions; they are of moderate length, moderate width, and moderate stiffness. Freeriders ride in a stiffer soft boot (some choose to ride in hard boots). Their stance is not quite sideways but also not quite facing the nose of the board—sort of in between.

Freestyle boot

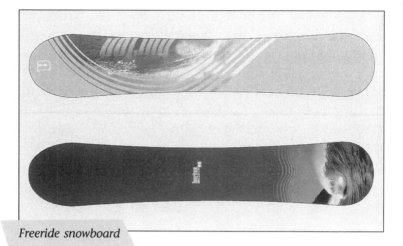

Freeride snowboard

Freeride boot

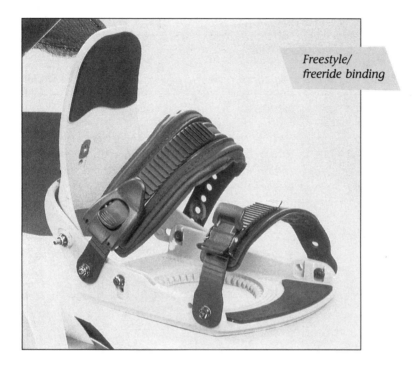

Freestyle/
freeride binding

What Do You Need to Know About Snowboards?

The questions that are most important to consider when choosing a snowboard are

1. What do I expect the snowboard to do (determined by riding style)?
2. What width snowboard do I need (which is determined by the size of your feet and the placement of your feet on the board)?
3. What length do I need (determined by your height and weight)?
4. How much flex do I need (determined by your strength)?

MEN'S SNOWBOARD SELECTION CHART

SMALLER MOUNTAINS	FREESTYLE
(less than 1,500' vertical	FREERIDE
mostly hard snow, parks, pipes)	EXTREME

FOOT SIZE (U.S. men's)	WEIGHT (lb.)	TRY THIS (board length and width)
9.5–14	more than 160	FS 150–160 cm, >25 cm
	130–160	FS 145–155 cm, >25 cm
5.5–9	more than 160	FS 150–160 cm, 24–25 cm
	130–160	FS 145–155 cm, 24–25 cm
	100–130	FS 140–150 cm, 24–25 cm
	less than 100	FS 130–140 cm, 24–25 cm
5 or smaller	100–130	FS 130–145 cm, <24 cm
	less than 100	FS 100–135 cm, <24 cm

FS = freestyle, FR = freeride, L = longboard

Different body types in combination with different desires will determine the appropriate length, width, and flex your snowboard should have, matching the best performance tool to you.

Where and how you ride will affect the ideal length snowboard you will need. Those who ride in deep powder a lot (Washington, Oregon, Colorado, Utah) will want a longer board, whereas someone who lives on the East Coast and rides hard-packed snow will want a shorter board. Someone who wants to just do freestyle tricks will

MEN'S SNOWBOARD SELECTION CHART

BIGGER MOUNTAINS
(more than 1,500' vertical
full range of terrain and snow conditions)

FREESTYLE
FREERIDE
EXTREME

FOOT SIZE (U.S. men's)	WEIGHT (lb.)	TRY THIS (board length and width)
9.5–14	more than 160	FR 155–165 cm, >25 cm
	130–160	FR 145–160 cm, >25 cm
5.5–9	more than 160	FR 155–165 cm, 24–25 cm
	130–160	FR 145–160 cm, 24–25 cm
	100–130	FR 140–155 cm, 24–25 cm
	less than 100	FR 130–145 cm, 24–25 cm
5 or smaller	100–130	FR 135–150 cm, <24 cm
	less than 100	FR 105–140 cm, <24 cm

*Men's Snowboard Selection Chart, reprinted from
Transworld Snowboarding Magazine, September, 1997.*

need a shorter board than someone who wants to ride big, steep mountains.

The ideal width of the snowboard is determined by your foot size. Your toes and heels should be directly over the toe and heel edges of the snowboard. If they hang more than a half-inch over, the board is too narrow. And if your foot doesn't overhang at all, the board is too wide. Having good leverage over the edges is important, as that's how you steer.

MEN'S SNOWBOARD SELECTION CHART

BIG MOUNTAINS/ BACKCOUNTRY   FREESTYLE
(more than 1,500' vertical   FREERIDE
mostly powder or softer snow)   EXTREME

FOOT SIZE (U.S. men's)	WEIGHT (lb.)	TRY THIS (board length and width)
9.5–14	more than 160	FR/L 160–180 cm, >25 cm
	130–160	FR/L 155–170 cm, >25 cm
5.5–9	more than 160	FR/L 160–180 cm, 24–25 cm
	130–160	FR/L 155–170 cm, 24–25 cm
	100–130	FR/L 145–160 cm, 24–25 cm
	less than 100	FR 140–155 cm, 24–25 cm
5 or smaller	100–130	FR 140–155 cm, <24 cm
	less than 100	FR 110–145 cm, <24 cm

FS = freestyle, FR = freeride, L = longboard

The flex of a snowboard refers to the resistance a board provides in a turn. Someone who is heavy and strong would need a stiff board that can remain stable in a turn. Someone who is lighter and not as strong won't be able to arc such a stiff board and would require a board with a softer flex.

The differences between snowboards are becoming less noticeable: ounces of difference in weight, millimeters of difference in sidecut, an oak wood core rather than a

MEN'S SNOWBOARD SELECTION CHART

ALL-MOUNTAIN FREECARVING   ALPINE RACE
(mixed snow conditions)

WEIGHT (lb.)	Type of TURNS	TRY THIS (board length)
less than 160 lb.	gs/sg—higher speeds	freecarve 160–165 cm
	slalom—slower speeds	freecarve 140–155 cm
more than 160 lb.	gs/sg—higher speeds	freecarve 160–170 cm
	slalom—slower speeds	freecarve 150–160 cm

HARD CARVING/RACING   ALPINE RACE
(mostly hard snow)

less than 160 lb	gs/sg—higher speeds	race 150–165 cm
	slalom—slower speeds	race 135–155 cm
more than 160 lb	gs/sg—higher speeds	race 160–180 cm
	slalom—slower speeds	race 150–160 cm

Men's Snowboard Selection Chart, reprinted from
Transworld Snowboarding Magazine, *September, 1997.*

poplar wood core. Small though they may be, these differences do have an effect on the ride of the board but can only be measured in feel. As a beginner to the sport and one who doesn't know what snowboarding should feel like, telling the difference between snowboards can be next to impossible.

WOMEN'S SNOWBOARD SELECTION CHART

Board Length Range   weight (lb.)

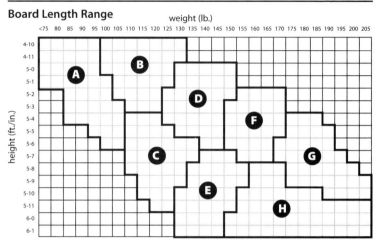

Find the letter that represents your weight and height. Then use the chart below to find the ideal board for your expected riding condition.

		Category 1	Category 2	Category 3
Riding Style/ Geographic Area		Deep powder Heavy snowfall areas Backcountry N. CA, ID, AZ, NM, OR, WA, AK, W. Canada	Groomed-trail resort riding Freeriding Light to moderate snowfall areas East Coast, Midwest, S. CA, E. Canada	Freestyle/tricks Halfpipe and park riding
Height/ Weight Class	A	130–145 cm	132–147 cm	134–149 cm
	B	134–149 cm	136–151 cm	140–155 cm
	C	138–155 cm	140–155 cm	142–157 cm
	D	140–155 cm	142–157 cm	144–159 cm
	E	142–157 cm	144–159 cm	147–162 cm
	F	144–159 cm	147–162 cm	150–165 cm
	G	149–164 cm	152–167 cm	155–170 cm
	H	151–166 cm	154–169 cm	160–175 cm

WOMEN'S SNOWBOARD SELECTION CHART

Board Width Range*

Foot Size (U.S. women's)	Freeride High Stance Angles	Freestyle Low Stance Angles
4 – 5½	22 cm	23 cm
6 – 6½	22.5 cm	23.5 cm
7 – 7½	23 cm	24 cm
8 – 8½	23.5 cm	24.5 cm
9 – 9½	24 cm	25 cm
10+	24.5 cm	25.5+ cm

*Widths refer to waist width.

Women's Snowboard Selection Chart, reprinted from Fresh and Tasty *magazine, October 1997.*

If all this is just too confusing, you can use this guideline: as a beginner, it is best to ride a board that is about nose high, made for turning (since that's what you need to be learning to do), allows a comfortable stance (feet about shoulder width apart), and is combined with a soft, forgiving set up (soft flexing board and soft boots). It is a good idea, for the first few times, to rent equipment until you get a feel for snowboarding so that you can begin to answer the questions about what you are looking for in a snowboard. After narrowing your choices, it is then best to choose a board from a company that has a reputation for quality, durability, and good customer service.

Expect to pay anywhere between $250 and $500 for a board without bindings. Just like anything else, variations in construction, production methods, and reputation will affect price. But most boards come with a one-year warranty and should see you through two seasons of heavy use or three moderate seasons. Those who don't plan on going more than five times might look to renting. Snowboard rentals range from $15 a day to full packages for $40. Call your local snowboard shop or resort to see what deals they have to offer.

What Do You Need to Know About Bindings and Boots?

Obviously, since the sport is called snowboarding, the snowboard is the main piece of equipment. Modern snowboard design has become standardized, with a fairly consistent core design and additional small innovations

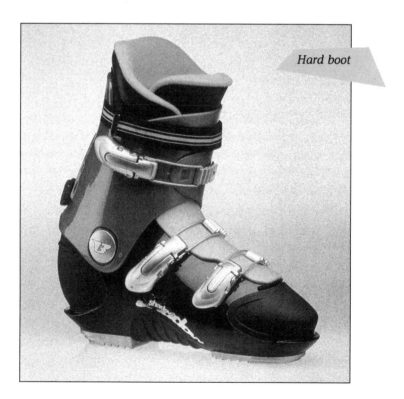

Hard boot

to improve durability. Greater attention now has been given to the improvement of board attachments and clothing. By board attachments, I mean the bindings and boots.

The most popular method of attaching a snowboard to oneself is by wearing soft snowboard boots and using strap/ratchet bindings. The reason most snowboarders are completely sold on snowboarding is because of the soft and comfortable snowboarding boot.

There are basically two types of boots: hard and soft. These different types of boots require different snowboard attachments, *i.e.*, bindings. Plates are used with hard boots and soft, ratchet/strap bindings are used with soft

Soft boot

boots. Hard boots with plate bindings are used for speed-oriented riding, *i.e.*, alpine. Hard boots are very similar to ski boots, except the boots are not quite as stiff and they allow for some lateral ankle motion. The bindings have a toe and heel bail that lock over the toe and heel of the boot. A very small percentage of riders use hard boots, and beginners looking for the "snowboard feel" should start out in soft boots.

Soft boots look like beefy snow boots with a bit of sneaker styling. They fit into soft, ratchet/strap bindings. Different models of boots will vary in stiffness, and which boot you'll be most comfortable in will be determined by how much ankle support you want. Stiffer boots provide more ankle support, and softer boots allow for maximum movement and flexibility.

The whole purpose of a snowboard boot is to fit comfortably while keeping your heel securely in the heel pocket, so that when you rock your weight from your heels to your toes, the board responds. Since no two feet are alike, even when they belong to the same person, fit is the most important determinant when choosing a pair of boots. Your choice should be the boot in which your feet feel the most comfortable.

The whole purpose of a binding is to fit snugly around your boot, keeping your foot attached to the board. Any movement of your boot within the binding translates to energy not transferred to the board but rather wasted, and that translates to you working harder without enjoying the results. While there are some differences between the traditional bindings offered, the only innovations offered concern ease of entry. The ratchet/strap binding design has been fairly stagnant over the past few years, as everyone has been focusing on the snowboard itself, but recently the design of the traditional snowboard binding has been receiving some attention from those who believe there just must be a better way! The search began for some innovative way to enable snowboarders to ride in a soft comfortable boot minus the archaic hassle of strapping on your board. Welcome to the step-in binding.

Step-in bindings were introduced in 1994 by K2 Snowboards, a subdivision of K2 Ski Corporation. As with snowboard development itself, there are some gray areas concerning who actually conceived of the first step-in binding, but while many people worked on the idea, it took K2 to bring it to the marketplace.

Since it is still a relatively new step in (I couldn't resist!) snowboarding technology, an industry standard has not yet been set, and there are many companies offering different meth-

Searching for a more convenient, more responsive ride, K2 introduced the Clicker step-in boot and binding system.

ods to achieve quick and easy in-and-out systems to attach you to your snowboard. A "newbie" to snowboarding should choose the most comfortable boot, and if it happens to be a step-in brand, then ride step-ins. If not, ride traditional bindings.

What Do You Wear?

The only snowboarding equipment left to discuss is snowboarding clothing. Protecting yourself from winter's wrath will make or break your snowboarding day. And dressing for snowboarding success is very simple. All you have to do is layer your clothing.

Long johns should be the first layer. The primary purpose of the first layer is to keep wetness from your skin; therefore, you want a fast-drying (for incoming wetness), wicking (for sweat) fabric such as polypropylene or silk. When snowboarding, even when the temperature is below freezing, you will sweat, and unless you don't have a wicking first layer, you will be freezing when you get back on the chairlift. Important: cotton is a no-no. When cotton gets wet it doesn't dry, and wetness next to your skin (surprise, surprise) does nothing to keep you warm. So no T-shirts!

Your top layer consists of a snow-wear jacket and snow-wear pants. The ideal top layer is waterproof so the snow's moisture won't seep in and is breathable so it doesn't cause you to sweat. This is a bit of a contradiction as nothing can be 100 percent waterproof and 100 percent breathable. For example, the ultimate waterproof fabric is rubber, but it's not breathable. Snowboarding clothes utilize fabrics and laminates in order to produce the most waterproof/breathable garment possible.

The weather conditions where you snowboard will dictate how technical your snowboard wear needs to be. (Southern California doesn't need powder skirts and hoods, but Vermont does.) Once the waterproof/breathable requirement is met, the only other decisions in choosing clothing are what fits and what you like. Different styles will offer different features, such as number of pockets, fabric flaps behind zippers to block the wind, hoods and hood adjustments, to name a few. But in choosing, remember the main function of your snowboard clothing is to keep you *warm* and *dry*.

What goes in between the first layer and the top layer depends on the weather and your own internal thermostat. Freezing and below-freezing temperatures will require at least two layers in between. The in-between layers should be of clothing made out of fleece or wool. Again, no cotton!!

To protect what snowboarding clothes do not, you will need to dress your hands, feet, neck, and head. A durable glove that keeps snow from getting in at your wrist is necessary, as your hands will come in contact with the snow. A hat and neck gaiter or scarf will block the wind and snow, and wool socks will keep those tootsies warm.

And lastly, don't forget to protect your eyes and skin. On sunny days the UV rays that are reflected off all that white snow can be very damaging to both your eyes and your skin. Sunglasses can be worn, but snowboarding goggles are designed to stay in place as well as to give you full-wrap protection that prevents intrusion injuries. And don't let the cold temperatures affect your decision to use sunblock.

You're all set. What are you waiting for? . . . Oh, you have more questions?! Right on. I mean read on.

"For the first-timer, take a lesson. You will save yourself some slams. Use good equipment that fits well. And it wouldn't hurt to wear a butt pad!"

Shannon Dunn

Shannon Dunn earning a living at Sierra-at-Tahoe

Age: 24

Years snowboarding: 8

Sponsor: Burton

Focus: Halfpipe competition

How it all began: "My older brother, Sean, taught me how to snowboard eight years ago, when Steamboat Springs, Colorado, first allowed snowboarding. It was a rough, fun day. Afterward, I was so sore, I could barely walk. The next time I went, I bought a board. It was a K2 Gyrator. My brother and I knew all the snowboarders then because there was just a small group of us—those were the days. (Ha! Ha!) I rode a lot with my brother, and we started going to the Rocky Mountain Snowboard Series Contests. I was going to CU-Boulder for the fall semester, and I was sure snowboarding was just a hobby. But one thing led to another, and I figured I should hold off on school until I could go both semesters and give 100 percent. So here I am, still snowboarding as my job, and I feel very lucky."

4

How Do You Learn to Snowboard?

Most snowboarders you talk to will tell you that it takes about three days to learn to snowboard. The hardest part is when you are introduced to your downhill edge. This will be the cause of many a fall. The primary challenge is to learn how a snowboard moves, and more important, how to move the snowboard to make it stop. As in many sports, the fear for most beginners is the fear of not being in control—in this case, not being able to stop.

Before snowboarding became so popular, beginners had to take their falls and figure the puzzle of the sport out on their own. There weren't very many people to watch, and instruction consisted of your friend saying, "Dude, just point it and go." But now there are a lot of snowboarding experts, so why not benefit from their knowledge rather than trying to reinvent the wheel? It is slow and extremely frustrating to try to learn on your own. *Take a lesson*, and watch and copy the experts.

Beginning to snowboard, unlike beginning to ski, is a little tricky. Skiing gives you independent movement of your legs and starts you off in a familiar stance: facing forward. With snowboarding, you have to get used to a different approach. Unless you have skateboarded or surfed before, controlling your movements from a sideways stance feels quite different.

Before you even begin, you should determine if you are more comfortable riding the board with your left foot forward or your right foot forward. Whichever foot is forward is responsible for initiating turns and supporting most of the weight. Those who feel more comfortable with their left foot up front are called "regular" riders, and those more comfortable with their right foot up front, "goofy" riders. Sometimes this decision is not quite fully worked out before the first lesson as some people change their mind halfway through. A good way to determine this is to slide sideways in your socks on a smooth floor;

The author, feeling like a superstar, heliboarding with Wasatch Powderbird Guides in Utah

whichever foot leads should lead for snowboarding too.

Being a beginner can be the best time in any new sport. Challenges are quickly mastered, and that superstar feeling of accomplishment is easy to achieve. Enjoy this time and relish all the first times. As you get more advanced, improvement is less noticeable.

Is There Snowboard-Specific Instruction?

Until recently snowboard instructors were certified by the ski organization Professional Ski Instructors of America (PSIA). Back in 1990 a snowboarding program was developed by the PSIA to provide "teaching certification" to snowboard instructors. As the demand for snowboard instructors and snowboard lessons increased, PSIA realized the need for a new education association dedicated specifically to snowboarding. The American Association of Snowboard Instructors (AASI) was established in 1997.

Following the same model as the PSIA, AASI organized methods of learning how to snowboard and developed drills to be used to teach snowboarding skills. Standardizing teaching methods is helpful so that you, the snowboarding student, can frequent different resorts and still find consistency in instruction. With rigorous requirements, the goal of AASI is to teach snowboard instructors how to identify what type of learner a new student is and to adapt instruction to that student's needs and learning style. Some students will need detailed explanation, others may need their bodies positioned so they can feel the movements, and still others may just need to watch the instructor's model. Explaining the skills in a way that is easily understood is very important.

What Can You Expect in a Beginner Lesson?

The first lesson introduces you to the snowboard and the basic concept of snowboarding; that is, "the snowboard slides down the hill and you need to keep your balance on it."

Once that is achieved, you need to begin controlling—that is, turning—the board. It is important to keep the majority of your weight on your front foot. As a beginner, you will find this a difficult skill to master because when you don't feel in control, you don't want to commit to the downward slope of the hill. You immediately

Pete Jacobs demonstrating a toeside turn: weighting his toes and setting the toeside edge of the board into the snow

want to stop. But momentum has to be attained before you can begin to learn control.

In your first lesson you will start off on a very gradual slope and begin with drills that teach you to trust your front foot and weight your front foot. This allows the snowboard to work with gravity and gain momentum as you proceed down the hill. Once that skill is mastered (usually a quarter to halfway through the first lesson), you will learn to weight the toeside and heelside edges, which allow you to steer.

After this introduction to the turning technique, the instructor will take you up the bunny slope so you can slide down the hill and practice steering with your newly found toeside and heelside edges.

Pete Jacobs demonstrating a heelside turn: weighting his heels and setting the heelside edge of the board into the snow

What Are Some Helpful Tips?

The experts make it look easy. You want to just jump on board and smoothly and effortlessly link turns down the mountain. But it takes some time and some practice until turning becomes second nature. The beginning lessons are all about embedding the snowboarding skills in your muscle memory so you don't have to waste all your brain power concentrating on control. So don't get frustrated. Set incremental goals and be proud of your progress.

The three universal hints to successful snowboarding are to keep your knees bent, to look to where you are going, and to listen to your instructor. Keeping your knees bent will help keep your muscles relaxed and ready to receive orders. Look to where you are going and not down at the snowboard and your feet. Looking ahead will help you steer and keep you prepared for upcoming obstacles. Ask your instructor questions. Benefit from her experience. And lastly (I know I said there were only three), Don't Fight It. The snowboard is supposed to move. It's actually much harder to stand on and stay balanced when it is perfectly still. The most difficult thing about being a beginner is giving up control in order to learn how to have control.

Will You Fall?

The reason that learning to snowboard (or almost any new sport for that matter) is difficult is because of the fear of falling, especially for adults, who usually do not fall very often! But falling is a skill. Your instructor will teach you how to fall and have you practice so that you will learn to fall well—using your knees and rolling rather than trying to catch the fall on your hands.

Plan to fall and be covered in snow. Wearing pads is a good idea: butt pads, knee pads, and a helmet. For the first few times out, be conscious of not catching your body weight on your hands. Fending off the ground with the strength of your wrist will most likely result in injury. Drop to your knees or your natural cushion—your butt—and roll with it.

Snowboarding is like learning to ride a bike. Gravity is your friend, and balance is easier to achieve at speed. And since you need speed to make the turns, you should plan to lose a little bit of control. It is for this reason that beginning to ski is easier than beginning to snowboard. With skiing, you can keep your balance at slower speeds because, like a bike with training wheels, you have a wider stance. But that habit of the "pie" stance is what you will spend the next umpteen lessons trying to break! To snowboard, you are taught the correct technique right off the bat.

How Many Lessons Will You Need?

Snowboarding is relatively easy to master. Once the skill of turning is achieved, snowboarders can feel free to discover the rest of the mountain on their own, pushing the limits to see what kind of terrain will threaten their control, taking steeper runs, and dodging obstacles in the trees. As with all skillful endeavors, the ultimate goal is being able to control this new piece of equipment. Now that you are confident and strong on this snowboard, you feel confident as you search out the backcountry for those epic powder turns. The fun is trying new and harder challenges and being able to "dew" it.

Beginner Class Overview*

Goals
Become familiar with equipment, new movements, and a new environment.
Learn the basics of skating, gliding, turning, and stopping.
Develop the sensations of moving and sliding.
Introduce side slipping and traversing.
Learn to vary speed by side slipping, basic turning, and stopping.
Develop group interaction, group dynamics, and experience the mountain environment.

Safety Considerations
Wear proper clothing, skin and eye protection.
Teach warm-up and stretching.
Show students how to carry and set board down.
Show students how to check equipment.
Work from flat terrain to steeper terrain gradually.
Show students how to get up after a fall.

Action Plan

1. Students feel out of place with a new sport. Make them feel welcome and comfortable with equipment, new sensations and the learning process.
2. Pick terrain that allows students to feel they have some degree of control.
3. Pace class relative to needs and abilities. Students should feel comfortable with the terrain and each exercise before moving on. Be aware of pushing the students too quickly to turn and to ride the lift. Students' expectations include attaining confidence in their ability to control the board and stop before going on to steeper terrain.
4. Take time to develop sound fundamentals which will lead to continued success.
5. Make sure students are comfortable walking and skating and can move uphill with good balance. Make sure students are developing basic edging and pressuring skills.
6. Emphasize how specific movement patterns produce specific results.

*Material courtesy of the American Association of Snowboard Instructors.

"*Try to do all your tricks in a logical progression. Get comfortable with what you can do and build from that. The little subtleties in the smaller moves are the keys to the bigger tricks. I go back to tricks I did years ago and try to do new things to them; shoulder gestures or the way you tilt your head can really make a trick different. And don't force it. Different people progress at different paces.*"

Todd Richards

Todd Richards at the American Pro Snowboard Series finals

Age: 27

Years snowboarding: 10

Sponsors: Morrow, Oakley, BC Surf & Sport

Focus: "Having fun"

How it all began: "I knew Rob Levine, back in 1985. He was the first to have a snowboard. I tried snowboarding for a little while and hated it because I could barely make the board go down the hill; I couldn't do any skateboard tricks. I dropped it for a couple of years, and then I went to college at the University of New Hampshire, near Gunstock. I snowboarded there a couple of times and had a good time."

5

What Tricks Can Snowboarders Do?

Why Do Tricks?

Tricks are created for two reasons: the desire to prove mastery of the skill and to just plain show off. Tricks are developed because just doing the basics is not challenging enough. Tricks are for those who want to push the limits, inspire awe in others, and contribute to the sport's style. Tricks are the decorations that attract attention.

While there are ground tricks, these are usually not as impressive and don't get the big crowd-pleasing points as do the tricks that are done in the air. The most common ground trick is to ride backward—in snowboarding terms, "fakie." For those who normally ride with their right foot forward, riding with their left foot leading would be "fakie." Riding fakie has now become a standard, and the pros do it so well that oftentimes it's difficult to tell which is their regular stance and which is fakie. As a result, they sometimes miss getting the extra difficulty points for taking off or landing an air trick backwards.

The most common air trick is just getting some! Getting air is awesome. Even if you just do a little hop, you get a brief taste of flying. And once you taste it, you will continue to try to make it last longer and longer. The big guns are now dropping fifty-foot cliffs and jumping over sixty-foot gaps. Snowboarding tricks have really reached stunt-level proportions.

The tricks the world will watch are tricks in the half-pipe, which will be an event in the 1998 Olympics. These tricks were derived from skateboarding. As a matter of fact, riding in a halfpipe was derived from skateboarding. The tricks snowboarders are doing are tricks that have been done on skateboards.

Okay, so the most basic trick is just getting air and, of course, the bigger the air, the more impressive the trick. Once the riders are in the air, they do something to show the spectator that they are in control, such as grabbing their board or posing in some stylish manner. Currently, standard tricks include monstrous airs while grabbing the board, spinning and grabbing the board, and even flipping, spinning, and then grabbing the board. The limits are constantly being pushed as riders mix airs, grabs, and spins.

All this starts getting too complex, especially if you aren't the one actually doing the trick. While it's more difficult to recognize the subtleties that differentiate one trick from another, it is easy to understand the basics.

What Tricks Are There?

Snowboarders are launching big airs, striking stylish poses, spinning, and flipping to prove their mastery of the sport. While this is certainly something to strive for, mastering the basics will only make you appreciate more what the pros and superstars of the sport are doing.

Straight Air

First, let's start off with getting air. Off a straight jump (aka a "kicker"), it's a matter of bending your knees and letting the kicker loft you up. It takes a bit of technique to push off the lip of the jump to get maximum air, but because it is a jump, no matter what you do, you will get air. The more speed and the bigger the jump, the "bigger" you will go. (See photos on pages 68–69.)

Halfpipe Air

Unlike an air off a straight jump, airing in the halfpipe actually includes a bit of a rotation. To reenter the pipe with the same foot leading as when you rode up the wall, you have to rotate 180 degrees (a half turn). Because there are two walls to the halfpipe, there are actually two

Tara Zwink demonstrating a frontside air—the front of her body is facing the wall of the halfpipe

Straight Air

Leigh Coates grabbing her heelside edge for a nice "method"

types of airs: a frontside air and a backside air. A frontside air means the front of your body is facing the wall; a backside air means your back is facing the wall.

Again, the more speed you carry up the wall, the higher in the air you will go.

At halfpipe contests, you see contestants soaring above the heads of the crowd. Typically, the walls of a halfpipe are about thirteen feet high, and snowboarders have been known to loft fifteen feet above that! Once you have reached your ultimate height, the next step is to start doing tricks while you're up there.

Anita Schwaller demonstrating a backside air—the back of her body is facing the wall of the halfpipe

Once you feel comfortable and confident skying above the lip, the next step is to try to grab your board in different places, to add some challenge.

Grabs

Grabs come from the world of skateboarding. Since skateboards don't stay attached to your feet, it was thought that you had to grab the board to keep it underneath you as you jump and land. Makes sense, right? But then Alan "Ollie" Gelfand discovered

Seth Neary keeps the skateboard under his feet without using his hands. It's not magic, but rather a certain way to jump to keep the skateboard moving with you. This jumping motion is called an "ollie."

that you could defy gravity by jumping a certain way to bring the skateboard with you beneath your feet without holding on to it.

This made a huge impact on the skateboarding world and added a whole new dimension to the tricks they could do, but for a lot of airs, they would still grab onto the skateboard. In snowboarding the board is attached to your feet, so there really is no reason to grab the board except that it looks cool. And grabbing the board shows control in the air; you look like you mean to be up there. Derived from existing skateboarding tricks, different grabs with different hands have different names. (See photos on pages 74–77.)

Grabbing the board on the toeside edge with your leading hand is a "mute"; the heelside edge with your leading hand is a "melancholy"; the toeside edge with your trailing hand is an "indy"; and the heelside edge with your trailing hand is a "stale fish." With each additional grab there is a new name, and only the pros who are performing the tricks can tell you the latest and greatest. And just when you begin to get a handle on the straight air tricks, the limits get pushed, and snowboarders start to spin.

Spinning

Nowadays it's all about spinning. The goal is to spin as many times as possible before you land. Rotations are measured in degrees. Facing north and then spinning all the way around to face north again is 360 degrees. Taking off the jump with your right foot forward, spinning all the way around so your right foot is forward again, is 360 degrees. Spinning only halfway around and landing fakie (backwards, remember?) is 180 degrees. All full rotations on a snowboard land you facing in the same direction from which you started, and half rotations land you fakie. (See photos on pages 78–81.)

Makes sense, seems logical. Now let me put a different "spin" on things. In the halfpipe, in order to continue riding in your forward stance (let's say right foot forward), you have to turn 180 degrees to lead with your right foot both up and back down the wall. Adding another half turn for a 360 leaves you riding backwards down the wall. This means that spins in the halfpipe are 180 degrees off the spins of straight kickers. In a halfpipe, all full rotations land you facing fakie, and half rotations land you back where you started. (See photos on pages 82–85.)

Flipping

Spinning, grabbing, lofting high in the sky—what more could there be? Well, there is always upside down. And not just run-of-the-mill back and front flips. These are back and front flips with rotations. I'm not kidding when I say that snowboarding has reached stunt-level proportions. (See photos on pages 86–89 and 90–93.)

The feats snowboarders accomplish are truly amazing. And with the beautiful backdrop of snow-covered mountains, people can't help but enjoy watching. And that's what many advertisers are counting on.

Grabs

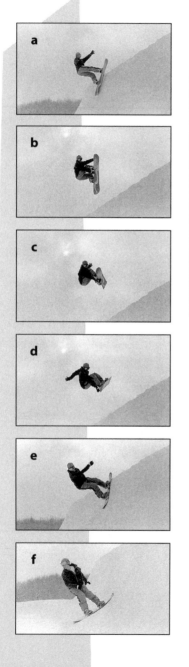

Cara-beth Burnside goes for the wacky "stale fish" grab.

Spinning

Jeremy Baye spins a full 360 degrees to land facing forward again.

John Sommers leads up the wall with his right foot, spins his board 360 degrees, and lands on the same wall leading with his left foot.

Spinning

Flipping

Rob Kingwill cleanly performs a "McTwist"—one and one-half rotations upside down!

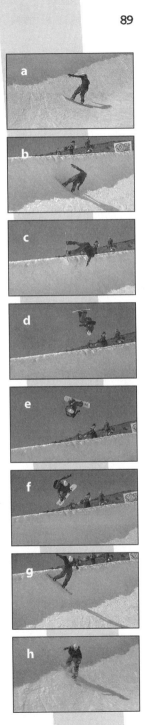

Flipping

A McTwist off a straight jump leaves you landing backward, or "fakie."

"*Snowboard competitions are pretty fun. Everyone out there is having a good time, hanging out with all your friends and having a good time, competing but not focused on winning. Why do I do it? Because it's fun, and you can also make a good living at it if you're pretty good. It takes a lot of hard work and training to be really good, but even if you're not, it's still a good time. The first competition I went to, everyone welcomed me right into it. Everyone was so outgoing. The people were so friendly, and everybody was having a good time. It was cool.*"

Travis McLain

Racing and half-pipe competitor Travis McLain getting stoked for his run at the 1997 U.S. Open

Age: 18

Years snowboarding: 5

Sponsors: Burton, Oakley, Dominator Wax

Focus: Alpine and halfpipe competition

How it all began: "I was a ski racer, and everyone was mean in ski racing. I did alright in skiing, but my spirit wasn't in it. It was too competitive and I was burnt. Everyone in snowboarding is nice, so I started snowboarding."

6

Are There Snowboarding Competitions?

Why Compete?

It's a proven fact that human beings love to play competitive games. So why not play some snowboarding games? We can play a game to see who can go the fastest. We can play a game to see who can jump the farthest. We can play a game to see who can do the most tricks. With this desire to participate in games, snowboarding competitions were born.

Ironically, many of the competitors in the early days explained their competitive interest as due to snowboarding's unpopularity. Snowboarding events opened up opportunities for riders with limited access to the slopes to have free reign over an area and to actually board on courses and obstacles set up specifically with snowboarders in mind. Ski resorts began to make an effort to cater to snowboarders by sponsoring competitions, and the snowboarders participated.

Another motivating factor was the camaraderie. A group of competitors became a tight group. Missing a competition meant missing fun. It wasn't an attitude of "I gotta go train, I gotta go train." It was more "Yeah, let's party, have fun." You won based on your natural abilities because people didn't train that much. Snowboarders were showing off in the halfpipe, improving their times, trying to learn new tricks, and pushing each other—creating the sport. The race courses, set in a controlled envi-

Tricia Byrnes performing before the crowd at the U.S. Open, Stratton, Vermont

ronment, provided an opportunity to go faster than you ever could freeriding. No ski patrol to warn you about slowing down; instead, fans cheering you to go faster.

But most important, competitions were *advertising*, plain and simple. If people weren't interested in watching you throw down tricks in a halfpipe on a cold, snowy day, there would be no money from sponsors. This scenario often prompts sighs of "sell-out"; for snowboarders, the greatest of all evils is to be mainstream. But from the early days of Burton, Sims, Avalanche, Gnu and Morrow, acceptance has been the goal. Snowboarding wouldn't be much fun on heavy wooden setups with metal fins and no bindings. Money was required for the innovations we snowboarders demanded. Competitions and the encouragement for professional riders provided the opportunity to fund the sport.

The 1983 World Snowboarding Championships at Soda Springs, Idaho, organized by Tom Sims, is recognized as having been the first true snowboarding competition because it included a halfpipe event. *Powder* magazine reported on this competition in its fall 1983 issue:

> *The first annual snowboard competition ever held drew an enthusiastic response from both competitors and sponsoring manufacturers ... Sliding, flying, spinning around the gates, over the jumps and through the bumps, the 28 best skiboarders in the country gave it everything they had in an attempt to prove their abilities in the three events: giant slalom, aerials, and freestyle. Amidst the whoops and hollers of the crowd, Tom Sims kept spinning down the slopes, eventually placing second overall.... Overall: 1. Scot Jacobsen 2. Tom Sims 3. Jake Burton.*

And an enthusiastic response is what the sponsors were looking for—publicizing the sport and bringing money into the industry, while bringing respect and worldwide recognition to the sport. Suddenly snowboarding had value, and Swatch, Op, Body Glove, Quiksilver and Suzuki all became sponsors of snowboarding competitions. The big dollar signs attracted the best riders, who showed off some spectacular riding, which brought more and more spectators, who brought more sponsors and more money and enabled snowboarders to earn a living snowboarding.

How Did Competitions Begin?

Back in 1979 Jake Burton Carpenter decided he wanted to play on his new and improved Snurfer with bindings, so he went to that year's annual Snurfer contest in Michigan. The organizers of the competition didn't take too kindly to his newfangled equipment and argued that he couldn't compete against the traditional binding-less Snurfer. Finally, after battling it out, it was decided to create a separate division in which Burton was the only entrant. Not surprisingly, he placed first in his division!

From that experience Burton put together his own snowboard competition: the U.S. Open. This event is the Big Daddy of events, the one that's a definite must. With the biggest media draw, the most spectators, and billed as the oldest and most prestigious event in the sport, the U.S. Open, held annually at Stratton Mountain Resort in Vermont, is one of the largest North American stops on the World Pro Tour.

The businessman in Jake Burton was intentionally aiming to draw attention to snowboarding and increase local interest and understanding of the sport. He hoped to encourage potential customers by pushing for local advertising and by keeping the finish lines close to the base area for spectators. The growing recognition of the sport encouraged other companies outside the industry (who individually had a lot more on their bottom line than the combined snowboarding industry) to organize events offering big prizes to lure the best riders.

Resorts began opening their doors to these new lift ticket purchasers, and the interest in snowboarding rapidly increased (just as Jake Burton Carpenter and Tom Sims had planned). Ocean Pacific in 1988 sponsored the "Op Aspen Grand Prix of Snowboarding." In 1990 Body Glove developed the Professional Snowboard Tour of America (PSTA) with eight events and $250,000 in prize money. In 1991 the PSTA created the Nissan Snow Tour with eight events and $80,000 in prize money, while 1993 saw the development of the American Pro Snowboard Series, including the Butterfinger Pro Snowboard Tour and 6th Annual Op Pro of Snowboarding. Bud Light entered the snowboarding craze in 1994 with two events: one in Bear Mountain, California, and one in Snowmass, Colorado. In 1994–95 ESPN and ESPN 2 produced seven television programs, and 1996 brought the designation of snowboarding as a Winter Olympic medal sport, scheduled to premiere in the 1998 Olympics in Nagano, Japan.

Is Snowboarding Going to Be in the 1998 Olympics?

Okay. What's all this talk about the Olympics? How can snowboarding, this fledgling sport, have quickly risen through the ranks to Olympic status? The requirements are very strict for acceptance into the Olympic "club."

Skateboarding and surfing haven't yet come near Olympic recognition, and yet snowboarding whisks right in? To be a recognized sport in the Olympics, a sport must be played by men in seventy-five countries over four continents, and by women in forty countries over three continents. In addition, the sport must have an international governing association and an established world championship event. Even if all these requirements are met, it still is up to the International Olympic Committee (IOC) board members to determine whether a sport will be included in the Olympics. The decision is based on factors such as: Is there room? Does it make sense? Is there worldwide interest? Are the athletes of Olympic caliber?

Does snowboarding meet all these demands? Well, at this time, no. At least not to the satisfaction of the International Olympic Committee. But skiing does. (This is the juicy part of the chapter.) Okay, here's the deal. You have to remember what competitions are truly about: *advertising.* This makes the Olympics the biggest commercial ever. For most sports the Olympics is their "Super Bowl," or even greater than that, because the audience is potentially, um, let me see . . . *the whole world!*

For many sports this is the goal: ultimate exposure, ultimate acceptance. And in 1990 Olympic dreams were being dreamed. Although the strict rules of the IOC made snowboarding's inclusion in the 1994 Winter Olympics in Lillehammer impossible, some did dream. Some were concerned that snowboarding was too young and that the influence of the big dollar signs might stifle the creativity and character of snowboarding. Would the Olympics provide the ultimate challenge for snowboarders or just the ultimate excuse to make fans of snowboarding watch hours of commercials in exchange for a few precious moments of boarding? Was the Olympics the direction snowboarding wanted to go, or should go?

The consensus in 1990 was that snowboarding needed time to mature. Olympic dreams were put on hold and attention given to standardizing event rules, establishing uniform judging criteria, and settling issues of professional vs. amateur status, as well as sponsorships and event requirements.

In 1991 Ted Martin of the United States, Christian Savio of Switzerland, and Kazuo Aguro of Japan established the International Snowboard Federation (ISF). The ISF is a snowboarding organization that was developed out of earlier predecessors of international competitive organizations to bring together an organization *for* snowboarders run *by* snowboarders—those who have a true passion for the sport. It of course makes sense that the people who get to decide the official rules are the people who play the game. It is also important that the provider of the rules have the best interest of the sport and competitors in mind—not solely financial gain. The goal of the ISF was to serve as a communication vehicle for the resorts, athletic organizations, and other groups that are important in the development of snowboarding. The ISF would also provide the rules and standards for snowboard competitions, including course requirements, judging guidelines, and competitor requirements, while also showcasing the sport and supporting its growth.

Meanwhile, the skiing community began to take notice of this sprouting new industry. *The Wall Street Journal* and *Newsweek* were reporting on the "fastest growing market" when describing snowboarding, and "decline worldwide" was the phrase associated with skiing. By 1994 the skiing industry realized they were missing out. At that year's biannual meeting of the Federation Internationale du Ski (FIS, the recognized governing body of skiing), a proposal was presented to take over the sport of snowboarding. The FIS began its own international snowboarding tour—after snowboarding had been scoffed at by the skiing community for so long. The ski industry decided it needed something to draw the most valuable snowboarders over to their side. The ploy . . . trumpets please . . . the golden entrance ticket to the Olympics.

How can skiing offer up the Olympics? Does the industry really have that much influence? Well, in a word, yes. Skiing already had met all the stringent requirements set forth by the IOC, and if snowboarding is considered an event under skiing, ruled and governed by the FIS, then, no problem. The IOC said "Voilà! Snowboarding is yours. As far as the Olympics are concerned, skiing owns snowboarding."

The price for participating in the 1998 Olympics in Nagano, Japan, is that skiing will own snowboarding. The FIS will decide the rules, the organization of competitions, and the judging standards. The FIS will determine which riders will make up the Olympic team. The FIS will have the authority to decide how snowboarding is presented to the world. And that's a lot of power.

It's true that snowboarding could choose to forge its own way, but we would have to get in line behind surfing, golf, chess, trampolining, stunt kite flying, and bowling, thus missing out on both the 1998 Olympics in Nagano as well as the 2002 Olympics in Park City, Utah. And it is unrealistic to think that the snowboarding industry can deny the urge to participate in the ultimate event. In spite of the hardcore and passionate snowboarders who may choose to remain loyal to snowboarding's desire for autonomy, the draw of the Olympics, the big dollar signs, and the tremendous opportunities brought on by the Olympics cannot be ignored.

What Are the Different Snowboarding Events?

RACE EVENTS
Super-G, Giant Slalom, Slalom

Early events included downhill ski events such as the slalom and the giant slalom (GS), as well as mogul competitions. Snowboarders either competed directly with skiers, or a separate division was created for this sideways-standing, pole-less group. These racing events are judged and organized just like their skiing counterparts. About the only difference is that the gates are designed differently to accommodate a snowboarder's stance.

A super-G is a relatively straight course at least 350 meters long, encouraging speeds in excess of 65 mph for up to two minutes. This is definitely a dangerous event and requires some guts. A giant slalom is set up with more gates on a smaller section of the mountain than a super-G, creating tighter turns that are more rhythmical. With more turning and shorter time to work with gravity, speeds are in the 45-mph range. The slalom (also called "parallel slalom") is a short sprinting course with tight gates that results in a quick-turning race that is run parallel (two riders on two courses). Slalom demonstrates a tight, controlled technique—being able to pull ahead in a sprint with a quick burst of energy. This event lasts less than thirty seconds.

FREESTYLE
Halfpipe, Slopestyle, Boardercross

In addition to the events adapted from skiing, snowboarders began to discover new ways to compare and compete against each other. The halfpipe event, which will be featured as one of the two events in the 1998 Olympics, is directly influenced by the skateboard crossovers, who have been riding metal and wood halfpipes since the '70s. A snowboard halfpipe is a U-shaped

A snowboard halfpipe

structure of snow; well, it's not really a structure, more like a ditch. A good halfpipe has walls of approximately thirteen feet with the top three feet at a 90-degree vertical angle to the ground. When you hit this wall at a good speed, you shoot straight up into the air. As you reach the height of your air, you prepare to re-enter the pipe using the same wall. The goal is to get as much air as possible (which is measured by the distance you reach above the top of the wall), do tricks while you are in the air above the top of the wall, and land with stability. If that all works out, aim toward the opposite wall and do it again.

Currently the halfpipe is judged like gymnastics and figure skating. Anywhere from four to five prominent people in the industry score the riders from 1–10, judging different elements: air, landing, spins, and grabs. The nature of the halfpipe requires subjective judging. This means that the judges have to be up on the latest and greatest tricks. And the problem is that nobody can be completely up-to-date on the latest tricks except the people actually doing the tricks. And the people who can actually do the tricks are the ones competing in the competitions, thus making the job of judge a tough one.

As the old saying goes, "only the winner is happy with the judging," and in a subjective event, it is unrealistic to think there is a solution that will change that. However, the search does continue to try to make the competition as fair as possible.

As snowboarding continued to grow into an individual sport rather than a skiing discipline, the search continued for events that better showcased riders. In 1992–93 slopestyle was introduced. This event, a judged event, better reflected what the snowboarders spent their days doing: riding the snowboarding park with their friends and throwing tricks over the tabletop jumps and gap jumps. The snowboarder takes the run individually, no timing involved, and makes her way through the tabletop jumps and gap jumps, throwing big grabs and "stylie" spins. The judges then award points on who gets the biggest air and performs the coolest trick. The official rules require that the slopestyle course contain at least one jump, one quarterpipe, and one wave site.

Another event, called boardercross, was inspired by snowboarders who ride the mountain with their friends, trying to snake each other for the first tracks, or trying to be the first over the jump. Introduced by those who were already into motocross, a course of banked turns, double and triple jumps, and whoops (no, not a mistake but rather a succession of small rollers meant to challenge the rider's balance) were designed. A heat of three to eight snowboarders vie for first place, usually at the expense of the other racers. The winner is the first one who crosses the finish line. Period. No extra points for great tricks, no deductions for falling.

Although these last two events don't have international point systems at the moment, which means you won't be seeing them in the Olympics, they are becoming standard events in the tour snowboarding competitions. What you will see in the Olympics is a racing event and a freestyle event—GS for racing and halfpipe for freestyle.

Taking risks and not doing things the same old way will help keep the spirit of snowboarding from being watered down by the mainstream. Snowboarding needs to continue to grow and define itself. This is a very important concern of the snowboarding community. Snowboarders want to preserve their passion for snowboarding, not just use it as a vehicle to win. They want to provide a fun event that all the best athletes will want to attend, to put on a spectacular competition so that the spectators will lose their pants watching, and to encourage the athletes to push the standards of the sport to limitless heights—creating respect and recognition around the world.

"Snowboarding in Japan is totally different from anywhere else in the world. They have one-person chairlifts that are really scary: a pole is attached to a little square piece of wood hovering twenty to thirty feet above the ground. It's super sketchy. But what's most interesting about snowboarding in Japan is that, at most of the resorts, the local belief is that the spirits of people who have died live in the trees, so they don't like you snowboarding in the trees—which is a big conflict with snowboarders who love to go in the trees on the powder days. I like to respect local customs, but it was hard, eyeing that stash, and Japan gets good snow. So, if you see those evil skull and crossbones signs that look like you're going to die and burn forever if you enter, remember even if that doesn't happen, the ski patrol will chase you down."

Lisa Kosglow

Lisa Kosglow

Age: 23

Years snowboarding: 8

Focus: Alpine racing

Accomplishments: AST 1997 Undefeated Tour Champion, 1st place 1997 U.S. Open.

How it all began: "A couple of my girlfriends found snowboards to ride so we went on the Bunny Hill at Bogus Basin in Boise, Idaho. I tried on the Burton Performer Elite 150 with tennis shoes. I was pretty much one of the first snowboarders at Bogus Basin, and because there weren't many girls doing it, I got to be the first one. One of my girlfriends kept up with it, and we started competing together in the Northwest. She went on the pro tour for a year and then burnt out and went to college, but I went on from there."

7
Where Do You Go Snowboarding?

Of course you should go snowboarding at the resorts. After all the work of gaining acceptance to ski resorts, present and future snowsliders can revel in the glory of breaking down the barriers. With chairlifts, groomed trails, professional instruction, and trained ski patrol for safety and first aid, resorts are made for snow-sliding fun. Resorts make snowboarding accessible and safe.

The biggest advantage of a resort (other than obviously the chairlift) is the resort's ski patrol, who keep an eye on avalanche conditions and help to keep the customer informed. Another advantage is trail markings to indicate dangerous terrain and obstacles. Currently each resort trail is marked according to steepness and difficulty: green (circle) = easiest; blue (square) = intermediate; black (diamond) = advanced (the more diamonds, the more advanced).

While these markings are helpful, they are only relative to the trails of the resort they mark, not to a standard scale. Typically, the intermediate trails out West would be marked as advanced trails in the East. Also, these markings were set up for skiing and indicate difficulty due to steepness and moguls. Unlike skiers, snowboarders don't seek out steep mogul trails. But we do love the trees, which unfortunately are also marked by double black diamond signs. This often leads to mistaken bump runs from hell.

Some resorts are changing their signage and adding snowboard ratings or snowboard maps. Rather than

Chairlifts, although the most important amenity, are just one of the many services offered by resorts.

using a difficulty rating, obstacle and jumping opportunities are noted. Maps also show flat trails to be avoided. Skiers can skate on flat trails, but snowboarders must release their back foot to push or walk. These helpful changes make the most of a day in the snow. (Be sure to ask if they have a snowboarding map when you buy your lift ticket.)

Yes, I said "buy your lift ticket." For all these amenities there's a price, of course. Lift ticket prices range from $35 to $42 U.S. Smaller resorts offering fewer trails and slower lifts will be less expensive than bigger resorts offering a variety of terrain, high speed chairlifts, and the works. Regardless of the ideal resort, you will spend the most time at the resort you have the closest access to. If it is not already, your local resort can become your ideal resort if you communicate your needs and wishes to them. As much as you want to keep buying a lift ticket, they want you to keep buying that lift ticket.

Where Do You Go Snowboarding?

The East Coast of the United States is known as the "Ice" Coast. The winter is fairly harsh but without a super amount of snow. While on the first day of a dump one can find light, fluffy snow, it is not a regular occurrence, and the terrain becomes icy and frozen over until the next snowfall. Powder days are not quite as frequent and require a little more effort and impulsivity to celebrate them. What the East does have on its side is the most technologically advanced skiing available. Armed with powerful snow-making machinery, the ski resorts can make their own fun if "Mr. Snowman" doesn't want to come out and play. And the lift service is unbeatable, with high speed chairs seating four to six people and gondolas to whisk you to the top.

The middle of the country doesn't have much of a reputation for snowboarding, because there aren't any mountains. There are a few hills that support cold enough temperatures to offer some winter snow-sliding fun, but the hills are not challenging enough to attract much outside interest. The locals are happy to have them, though, to satisfy their craving.

The West is touted as "The Best," and the western United States boasts favorite skiing destinations such as Colorado, Utah, Idaho, Montana, Oregon, and California. Regular snowfall accumulation tends to be five times that of the East. The terrain is bigger; the trees are bigger. The downside is that bigger does mean more dangerous. The West is also at the complete mercy of winter's storms, and its resorts don't have the snow-making capabilities of the East. But the West is not as densely populated, so the irregular, deep snow that does fall doesn't get as tracked up. There are many arguments over which coast offers the best season. The best scenario would be to ride everywhere. Variety is a beautiful thing! (See Appendix 1.)

Don't forget that Alaska is part of the United States, and snowboarding there is insane. As the weather conditions are extreme and unpredictable, snowboarding there is truly challenging. Alaska boasts the most skiable terrain in the entire United States—actually it has more skiable terrain than the other states put together. In spite of this, Alaska only has two resorts with traditional chairlift access, Alyeska and Eaglecrest. But helicopter charters are very easy to arrange, which makes much of the skiable terrain accessible. The most popular nonchairlift resort is Valdez, home of many extreme championship events (both snowboarding and skiing). This resort provides helicopter service to the Chugach Mountain Range.

Canadian terrain is similar to U.S. terrain and follows the same weather patterns. Eastern Canada corresponds to the eastern United States, western Canada to the western U.S. Even though farther north, the eastern coast of Canada is fairly warm and relies heavily on snowmaking, even more so than do New England's skiing resorts. The Quebec region in central Canada supports more snow due to the colder weather and has slightly higher elevations than one can find in the East.

As in the U.S., Canada's West is the Best. Boasting up to four hundred inches of snow annually, Alberta's Canadian Rockies offer forty-plus ski areas. The Banff/Lake Louise area has the largest amount of skiable terrain above the treeline. And in the province of British Columbia, the most talked about and visited resort is Whistler. Located on a glacier, Whistler is able to offer year-round skiing.

And if you don't think the mountains in the West are big enough, go to Europe. There, the mountains are huge. Unlike in the United States, the patrol is not as tight, which, on the one hand, means you can go pretty much wherever you want; on the other hand, however, you also could easily find yourself in danger. The lift service in Europe is still fairly outdated, with many surface lifts. Some lifts in distant snowboarding destinations have nicknames, like the New Zealand "nutcracker," which has you holding onto what looks like a nutcracker that is attached to a rope tow that runs you by big towers to pull you up the mountain. The more exotic your travels, the more prepared and educated you need to be. Don't be fooled into thinking that this beautiful sport is harmless. Be smart.

Speaking of exotic, even though snowboarding is a seasonal sport, when it is summer here in the U.S., it is always winter somewhere else. For example, Chile, New Zealand, and Australia all celebrate Christmas in the summer and Mother's Day in the early winter. And the glaciers of Mt. Hood, Oregon, and Whistler, British Columbia, hold snow into the late summer months of July and August.

Where Can You Snowboard Besides Resorts?

Resorts have a lot to offer: convenient, comfortable access to the tops of mountains, no work required on your part; safe, open trails; food and lodging nearby. And they are responding to the desires of their snowboarding customers. Halfpipes and terrain parks with jumps to loft you high in the air are regular additions at nearly every resort across the country.

More and more tree runs are being opened up to challenge the snow charger. But the steep and deep still lures the adventurer.

If terrain that everyone can access from the resort's chairlift isn't enough to satisfy your urge for fresh powder, you will need to look to alternative, less frequented methods of getting to the "stash." Hiking can get you some fresh turns. But to get where you want to go faster and with less physical demand, snowmobiles, snowcats, and helicopters can be hired. Just remember, as soon as you begin to venture off into untracked territory, you are increasing the chances of getting into danger.

Hiking, of course, is the cheapest method of getting to the stashes; it is also the most grueling. When out in

Matt Gormley, designer and manager of the "Boneyard" snowboard park at Waterville, New Hampshire, looks like he's right at home.

the backcountry, it is a must to travel in pairs, carry a shovel, use an avalanche transceiver, and have first aid items. Carrying this stuff up the mountain along with your snowboard is a lot of work. So consider the alternative. If you want to get those solitary turns without the hike, use a snowmobile, a snowcat, or a helicopter to whisk you up to those unpopulated areas. (See Appendix 2.)

"To avoid injury, it is important to stretch before snowboarding. It also helps to not be scared or tense. The more relaxed you are, the more likely your body will naturally react to a fall, keeping you from getting injured. In addition to staying relaxed, be aggressive but be in control."

Michele Taggart

Michele Taggart

Age: 27

Years snowboarding: 9

Sponsors: Salomon, Bonfire, Gargoyle Spoon

Focus: Halfpipe competition/freeriding

Snowboarding accomplishments: Four times Overall World Champion (1993–96).

How it all began: "I had skied for a long time, and my brother started snowboarding, so I decided to copy him. I would just follow him and his friends around."

8
Is Snowboarding Dangerous?

Is snowboarding dangerous? In a word . . . sure! Like all sports, getting hurt is always a possibility. And in addition to the risk of normal sports injuries, snowboarding is done in the winter. Winter weather is dangerous—the cold and snow have their own unique set of risks. However, it is possible to minimize those risks with proper attire and attitude.

The dangers of winter weather include getting buried under the snow and suffering frostbite (the freezing of some part of the body). Where you go snowboarding will determine how prepared for Mother Nature you will have to be. Snowboarding at a resort is relatively safe, and staying within the skiing boundaries will keep you from avalanche danger, 99 percent of the time. While you still have to dress to protect yourself from frostbite, civilization is close at hand. Therefore, it is just a matter of using good judgment and knowing your limits to keep yourself out of danger.

As a beginner, when it comes to snowboard safety, being out of control and falling is your biggest concern. But staying within your limits will keep the risks down. As a beginner, you will start on a mellow bunny slope, without obstacles, so you can focus on just gaining control. Still, being out of control on a mountain can be pretty scary. The greatest concern is not breaking your wrist(s). Many people put their hands down when trying to fend off a fall; no matter what kind of protective wrist gear you are wearing, your arm cannot support the weight of your fall. Your knees and butt are also in danger of bruising when you fall. Obviously, try not to collide with anything. And the last lesson here, which will be the first lesson when learning to snowboard, is Don't Catch Your Downside Edge. Doing this causes you to come to a complete stop, slamming you to the ground—it's kind of like throwing an anchor into the snow. It will only take a few experiences like this to convince you to keep your weight off the downhill edge.

Getting over the fear of falling will give you more confidence, making it less likely that you will fall. So wear knee pads and butt pads and spend some time practicing falling so that when you lose control, you won't fight the fall. Fortunately, the snowboard stays attached to your feet, so you are always in the position of feet being shoulder width apart, which will keep your body from getting tangled in some weird position.

Keep in mind that the harder packed the snow, the harder the fall. For this reason, plan to learn to snowboard when the snow conditions are good. Even if you have everything arranged and are prepared to commit to a lesson, if the snow is superfirm, postpone. Since the softer the snow, the easier the fall, try to save that first lesson for powder conditions. Powder gently invites you to try snowboarding!

Know how far you can push yourself without endangering yourself, use good judgment, take a lesson the first time you go out, dress properly, and make friends so you can keep an eye on each other. Keep your body hydrated, and stretch before and after riding. After all, it is exercise. Remember, no matter how good you get, Mother Nature still has the upper hand. Read this last section and make yourself a promise that if you begin leading your own expeditions to unknown destinations, you will get the proper education (first aid, avalanche recovery and rescue) and physical training to hold your own against the winter weather.

What Are Avalanches?

Avalanche injuries and fatalities are becoming more commonplace as a variety of winter sports become more accessible to those who are not well educated in winter dangers. Snowshoes and snowmobiles allow anyone access to avalanche prone terrain. And now snowboards can be included on that list. Those who snowshoe, snowmobile, and snowboard are the ones who are putting themselves at risk, searching for the stashes of untracked "pow." Fortunately, there are precautions to take to minimize the danger, the first of which is to know what you are dealing with.

Avalanches are caused by a weak layer in the snowpack. This weak layer slides under the weight of the snow on top of it, picking up more snow as it roars down the mountain and takes down everything in its path. Setting your snowboard edge into the snow can cause the snow to break loose and slide down the mountain. (Remember, snow is slippery.) This is pretty scary stuff; however, resort riders rarely experience avalanche accidents, and ski resorts in the high risk areas (the Rockies, Cascades, and Sierra Nevada ranges) regularly patrol the area, conducting snow tests and setting off explosives to settle the snow.

Liam Barrett taking a painless fall

Avalanche danger is more commonly encountered by those hiking to untouched stashes of pow outside the ski resorts' boundaries or riding on closed trails.

Deep snow can also be dangerous. Snow, like its cousin, water, can make breathing impossible. Tree wells are the most common places for people to "drown" in the snow. The branches of trees protect the trunk and sur-

*An avalanche
in action*

rounding ground from accumulating snow. As you get farther from the trunk of the tree, the snow gets deeper—creating a well around the tree. Falling in could leave you stuck with no way to get out. And most of the time, people who fall, fall in head first.

Until you become knowledgeable about winter precautions, it is not recommended that you venture away from patrolled areas or off resort trails.

There are courses that teach you avalanche safety: how to use a transceiver and probe so that if someone gets buried you can find them (a little like using a metal detector when looking for lost valuables in the sand at the beach). First aid courses are a must to teach you how to deal with emergencies while you are out in the wilderness. Take these precautions seriously. Even riding off the resort trail and into the trees right next to the trail could leave you with more than you bargained for.

Avalanche Schools and Seminars

Alaska Avalanche School
Anchorage, AK
(907) 345-3566

National Avalanche School/
National Avalanche Foundation
Lakewood, CO
(303) 988-1111
www.nsp.org
www.aasi.org

Silverton Avalanche School
Silverton, CO
(970) 387-5531

National Avalanche Center
Ketchum, ID
(208) 622-5371

American Association of Avalanche Professionals
Bozeman, MT
(406) 587-3830
www.avalanche.org

Sierra Ski Touring Winter Skills Series
Gardenville, NV
(702) 782-3047

American Avalanche Institute
Wilson, WY
(307) 733-3315

Canada

Canadian Avalanche Training School
Revelstoke, BC
(604) 837-2435
www.avalanche.ca/snow

Conclusion

You are now officially "in the know" when it comes to snowboarding. And while this may seem like just the tip of the iceberg, it actually is quite a solid foundation. Now the next step is to actually try it. As much as you may have enjoyed reading about snowboarding, actually doing it is ten times better!

Listen . . . you can hear the mountains calling you. Put down the book, pick up your snowboard, and get set for the ultimate ride!

Appendix

1

What Are the Best Resorts?

Of course you'll snowboard most often at the resort that is closest to your home, but for those yearly vacations arrange to check out the best the country has to offer. Based on my traveling experiences, these are the resorts that offer the best terrain (either natural or man-made), snow conditions, and amenities—in that order. Listed by state are my favorite resorts in the East and the West. Bon voyage, and may the pow be with you.

Top 15 in the East	Vertical Drop	Snowboard Park	Halfpipe
Sugarloaf USA, ME (207) 237-2000 www.sugarloaf.com	2,820 feet	yes	yes
Sunday River, ME (207) 824-3000 www.sundayriver.com	2,340 feet	yes	yes

Top 15 in the East	Vertical Drop	Snowboard Park	Halfpipe
Loon Mt., NH (603) 745-8111 www.loonmtn.com	2,100 feet	yes	yes
Waterville Valley, NH (603) 236-8311	2,020 feet	yes	yes
Hunter Mt., NY (518) 263-4223 www.huntermtn.com	1,600	yes	yes
Ski Windham, NY (518) 734-4300 www.skiwindham.com	1,600 feet	yes	yes
Whiteface Mt., NY (518) 946-2223 www.orda.org	3,216 feet	no	no
Seven Springs, PA (800) 452-2223 www.7springs.com	750 feet	yes	yes
Jay Peak, VT (800) 451-4449 www.jaypeakresort.com	2,153 feet	no	yes
Killington, VT (800) 621-MTNS www.killington.com	3,150 feet	yes	yes

Top 15 in the East	Vertical Drop	Snowboard Park	Halfpipe
Mount Snow, VT (800) 245-SNOW www.mountsnow.com	1,700 feet	yes	yes
Okemo Mt. Resort, VT (802) 228-4041 www.okemo.com	2,150 feet	yes	yes
Stowe, VT (802) 253-3000 www.stowe.com	2,360 feet	yes	yes
Stratton, VT (800) STRATTON www.stratton.com	2,003 feet	yes	yes
Sugarbush, VT (802) 583-2381 www.sugarbush.com	2,650 feet	yes	yes

Top 15 in the West	Vertical Drop	Snowboard Park	Halfpipe
Kirkwood, CA (209) 258-6000 www.skikirkwood.com	2,000 feet	yes	no
Mammoth Mt., CA (888) 4MAMMOTH www.mammoth-mtn.com	3,100 feet	yes	yes

Top 15 in the West	Vertical Drop	Snowboard Park	Halfpipe
Squaw Valley USA, CA (916) 583-6985 www.squaw.com	2,850 feet	yes	yes
Arapahoe Basin, CO (888) ARAPAHOE	2,250 feet	no	no
Copper Mt., CO (970) 968-2882 www.ski-copper.com	2,601 feet	yes	yes
Steamboat, CO (970) 879-6111 www.steamboat-ski.com	3,600 feet	yes	no
Sun Valley, ID (208) 622-6151 www.sunvalley.com	3,100 feet	no	no
Big Sky, MT (406) 995-5000 www.bigskyresort.com	3,030 feet	yes	no
Mount Bachelor, OR (800) 829-2442 www.mtbachelor.com	3,100 feet	yes	yes
Mount Hood Meadows, OR (503) 337-2222 www.skihood.com	2,777 feet	yes	yes

Top 15 in the West	Vertical Drop	Snowboard Park	Halfpipe
Brighton, UT (800) 873-5512 www.skibrighton.com	1,745 feet	yes	yes
Snowbird Resort, UT (801) 742-2222 www.snowbird.com	3,100 feet	no	yes
Solitude, UT (801) 534-1400 www.skisolitude.com	2,030 feet	no	no
Mount Baker, WA (360) 734-6771 www.mtbakerskiarea.com	1,500 feet	no	no
Jackson Hole, WY (307) 733-2292 www.jacksonhole.com/ski	4,139 feet	no	yes

2

Where Can You Snowboard Besides Resorts?

Heliboarding

United States

Alaska Air West
Kenai, AK
(907) 283-9354

Telluride Helitrax
Telluride, CO
(970) 728-4904

Sun Valley Helicopter Guides
Sun Valley, ID
(208) 622-3108

Montana Powder Guides
Bozeman, MT
(406) 587-3096

Ruby Mountain Heli-Ski
Lamoille, NV
(702) 753-6867

Wasatch Powderbird Guides
Utah Powderbird Guides
Snowbird, UT
(801) 742-2800

North Cascade Heli-Skiing
Winthrop, WA
(800) 494-HELI
www.methow.com/~heli-ski

High Mountain Heli Skiing
Teton Village, WY
(307) 733-3274

Canada

Assiniboine Heli Tours
Cranmore, AB
(403) 678-5459

Canadian Mountain Holidays
Banff, AB
(403) 762-7100

Mike Wiegele Helicopter Skiing
Banff, AB
(403) 762-5548

Crescent Spur Helicopter Skiing
Crescent Spur, BC
(250) 553-2300

Great Canadian Heliskiing
Golden, BC
(250) 344-2326

Kootenay Helicopter Skiing
Nakusp, BC
(250) 265-3121

Purcell Helicopter Skiing
Golden, BC
(250) 344-5410

R.K. Heli-Ski Panorama
Invermere, BC
(250) 342-3889
www.rkheliski.com

Robson Heli-Magic
Valemount, BC
(250) 566-4700

Mountain Heli-Sports
Whistler, BC
(604) 932-2070

Whistler Heli-Boarding
Whistler, BC
(604) 932-4105
www.whistler.net/resort/activities/whisheli/

Catboarding

United States

Aspen Mountain Powder Tours
Aspen, CO
(800) 525-6200

Great Divide Snow Tours
Monarch Ski Resort
Monarch, CO
(800) 228-7943

Irwin Lodge
Crested Butte, CO
(970) 349-9800

Steamboat Powder Cats
Steamboat Springs, CO
(303) 879-5188

The Big Mountain Snowcat Powderskiing
Whitefish, MT
(800) 858-5439
www.bigmtn@bigmtn.com

Mount Bailey Snowcats
Diamond Lake, OR
(800) 733-7593
www.mountbailey.com

Powder Mountain
Eden, UT
(801) 745-3771

Grand Targhee Snowcats
Alta, WY
(800) TARGHEE
www.grandtarghee.com

Canada

Great Northern Snowcat Skiing
Calgary, AB
(403) 287-2267
www.greatnorthernsnowcat.com

Cat Powder Skiing
Revelstoke, BC
(250) 837-5151

Island Lake Lodge
Fernie, BC
(250) 423-3700
www.mountainzone.com/islandlk

Selkirk Wilderness Skiing
Golden, BC
(250) 366-4424

Snow Much Fun Catskiing
Cranbrook, BC
(250) 426-5303

3

How Can You Learn More About Snowboard Adventures?

I f you just can't stop reading and need to know more, there is a wealth of information available to the inquiring snowslider. For personal interaction with other like-minded fans, camps and resort weekend events offer on-snow lessons and evaluations, new equipment demos, and lectures on equipment maintenance. There are also many magazines that cover the sport of snowboarding from a variety of focuses: a women's magazine, a men's magazine, a strictly East Coast magazine, etc. From there you will be opened up to a whole world of snowboard enthusiasts.

Magazines

Eastern Edge
Burlington, VT
(802) 297-3432
(target audience: East Coast snowboarders)

Fresh and Tasty
Cambridge, MA
(617) 547-6520
www.freshandtasty.com
(target audience: women)

Heckler
Sacramento, CA
(916) 444-8200
www.heckler.com
(target audience: hardcore snow/skateboarders)

Snowboard Canada
Toronto, ON
(800) 223-6197
(target audience: Canadians)

Snowboard Life
Oceanside, CA
(760) 722-7777
www.twsnow.com
(target audience: adult "mainstream")

Snowboarder
San Juan Capistrano, CA
(714) 496-5922
(target audience: men)

Stick
Santa Monica, CA
(310) 828-0522
(target audience: men)

Transworld Snowboarding
Oceanside, CA
(760) 722-7777
www.twsnow.com
(target audience: men)

Snowboarding OnLine ("SOL")
www.solsnowboarding.com
AOL Keyword: Snowboarding

Snowboard Camps

WINTER

United States

Delaney Camps
Boulder, CO
(303) 443-6868
www.Delaneysnowboard.com

Women Only Ski Camps
Warren, VT
(800) 451-4574
www.snowevents.com

Wild Women's Snowboard Camp
Jackson Hole, WY
(307) 734-5154

Canada

Jennie McDonald & Craig Kelly's Backcountry Camp
Island Lake Lodge, BC
(250) 423-3700
www.mountainzone.com/islandlk

SUMMER

United States

Rocky Mountain Snowboard Camp
Winter Park, CO
(970) 879-9059
www.rockysnocamp.com

High Cascade Snowboard Camp
Mount Hood, OR
(800) 334-4272
www.highcascade.com

Mount Hood Snowboard Camp
Mount Hood, OR
(503) 693-6725

Mount Hood Summer Ski Camp
Mount Hood, OR
(503) 337-2230
www.teleport.com/~skicamp

Windell's Snowboard Camp
Mount Hood, OR
(800) 765-7669

United States Snowboard Training Center
Mount Hood, OR
(800) 325-4430

Canada

Snowboard Camp of Champions
Whistler, BC
(604) 938-3450

Index

Chugach Mountain Range, 117
Clothing, 48–49
Coates, Leigh, *69*
Competitions, 94–109. *See also* Olympics
  as advertising, 99
  events, 105–109
  origins, 99–101
  reasons for, 97–100
Control, 58

Dakides, Tara, *7*
Derrah, Dave, 18
Derrah, Steve, 17
Dunn, Shannon, 50, *51*
  snowboard of, *6*

East coast snowboarding, 115
Equipment, 9–10, 31–49. *See also specific types*
  for alpine category, 31–33, *32, 33*
  clothing, 48–49
  for freeride category, 35–36, *36*
  for freestyle category, 33–34, *34, 35*
European snowboarding, 117

Falling, 58–59, 124, *126–127*, 129
Federation Internationale du Ski (FIS), 104
Feet positions, 54
Flipping, 73, *87–93*
  "McTwist," *87, 91*

Freeride, 11
  equipment, 35–36, *36*
Freestyle, 11
  boardercross, 108–109
  equipment, 33–34, *34, 35*
  halfpipe, 66, 67–68, 70, *106,* 106–107
  slopestyle, 107–108
Fresh and Tasty, ix

Gelfand, Alan "Ollie," 71
Giant Slalom, 105
Goggles, 49
Gormley, Matt, *119*
Grabs, 71–72
  "indy," 72
  "melancholy," 72
  "mute," 72
  "ollie," 71
  "stale fish," 72, *74–77*
Grell, Jeff, 17, *26,* 26–27

Heliboarding, 139–141
Hiking, 118–119

"Indy," 72
Instructors, 55
International Snowboard Federation (ISF), 103

Jacobs, Pete, *56, 57*
Jacobsen, Scot, 99
Japan, 110

K2 Ski Corporation, 47
Kingwill, Rob, *87–93*
Kosglow, Lisa, 110, *111*
Kunkel, Rol, *4*